Dato 3/10 £21.99

Institute of Leadership
& Management

Lea **uperseries**

Don'
belc
thrc

I pre

Managing
Performance

FIFTH EDITION

Published for the
Institute of Leadership & Management

AMSTERDAM • BOSTON • HEIDELBERG • LONDON • NEW YORK • OXFORD
PARIS • SAN DIEGO • SAN FRANCISCO • SINGAPORE • SYDNEY • TOKYO
Pergamon Flexible Learning is an imprint of Elsevier

ELSEVIER

Pergamon
Flexible
Learning

Pergamon Flexible Learning is an imprint of Elsevier
Linacre House, Jordan Hill, Oxford OX2 8DP, UK
30 Corporate Drive, Suite 400, Burlington, MA 01803, USA

First edition 1986
Second edition 1991
Third edition 1997
Fourth edition 2003
Fifth edition 2007

Copyright © 1986, 1991, 1997, 2003, 2007 ILM. Published by Elsevier Ltd. All rights reserved

Editor: David Pardey

Based on material in previous editions of this work

The views expressed in this work are those of the authors and do
not necessarily reflect those of the Institute of Leadership &
Management or of the publisher

British Library Cataloguing in Publication Data
A catalogue record for this book is available from the British Library

Library of Congress Cataloguing in Publication Data
A catalogue record for this book is available from the Library of Congress

ISBN 978-0-08-046429-9

For information on all Pergamon Flexible Learning publications
visit our website at http://books.elsevier.com

Institute of Leadership & Management
Registered Office
1 Giltspur Street
London
EC1A 9DD
Telephone: 020 7294 2470
www.i-l-m.com
ILM is part of the City & Guilds Group

Typeset by Charon Tec Ltd (A Macmillan Company), Chennai, India
www.charontec.com
Printed and bound in Great Britain

07 08 09 10 11   10 9 8 7 6 5 4 3 2 1

Contents

Workbook introduction

Session A Measuring performance

Session B Monitoring and improving performance

Series preface

Whether you are a tutor/trainer or studying management development to further your career, Super Series provides an exciting and flexible resource to help you to achieve your goals. The fifth edition is completely new and up-to-date, and has been structured to perfectly match the Institute of Leadership & Management (ILM)'s new unit-based qualifications for first line managers. It also harmonizes with the 2004 national occupational standards in management and leadership, providing an invaluable resource for S/NVQs at Level 3 in Management.

Super Series is equally valuable for anyone tutoring or studying any management programmes at this level, whether leading to a qualification or not. Individual workbooks also support short programmes, which may be recognized by ILM as Endorsed or Development Awards, or provide the ideal way to undertake CPD activities.

For learners, coping with all the pressures of today's world, Super Series offers you the flexibility to study at your own pace to fit around your professional and other commitments. You don't need a PC or to attend classes at a specific time – choose when and where to study to suit yourself! And you will always have the complete workbook as a quick reference just when you need it.

For tutors/trainers, Super Series provides an invaluable guide to what needs to be covered, and in what depth. It also allows learners who miss occasional sessions to 'catch up' by dipping into the series.

Super Series provides unrivalled support for all those involved in first line management and supervision.

Unit specification

Title:	Managing performance		Unit Ref:	M3.26
Level:	3			
Credit value:	I			

Learning outcomes The learner will	Assessment criteria The learner can (in an organization with which the learner is familiar)	
I. Know how to manage performance	I.I	Briefly explain the role of the First Line Manager in performance management
	I.2	Set SMART objectives for the team
	I.3	Set performance standards for the team
	I.4	Explain how you would measure performance against agreed standards
	I.5	Select an example of underperformance in the workplace and explain a performance improvement technique available to address this underperformance

Workbook introduction

1 ILM Super Series study links

This workbook addresses the issues of *Managing Performance*. Should you wish to extend your study to other Super Series workbooks covering related or different subject areas, you will find a comprehensive list at the back of this book.

2 Links to ILM qualifications

This workbook relates to the learning outcomes of Unit M3.26 Managing Performance from the ILM Level 3 Award, Certificate and Diploma in First Line Management.

3 Links to S/NVQs in management

This workbook relates to the following Units of the Management Standards which are used in S/NVQs in Management, as well as a range of other S/NVQs:

Unit D6: Allocate and monitor the progress and quality of work in your area of responsibility.

4 Workbook objectives

As a first line manager, you may be expected to meet budgetary targets, expressed in financial terms. But very detailed 'performance' targets are often much more practical, such as 'serve 20 customers per hour', or 'inspect five junction boxes per day'. This workbook is intended to help you understand how to meet performance targets, and agree targets that are realistic.

4.1 Objectives

When you have completed this workbook you will be better able to:

- identify ways of measuring performance levels;
- describe a range of methods for measuring performance;
- identify the differing objectives of stakeholders in the organization;
- identify and agree performance objectives with the members of your work team;
- select the ideal performance measure;
- monitor performance against agreed targets;
- make recommendations for improvement in performance, or adjustments to more realistic targets.

5 Activity planner

The following Activities require some planning so you may want to look at these now.

- Activity 25 – where you use the balanced scorecard to suggest improvement.
- Activity 29 – in which you gather information for measuring performance.
- Activity 35 – which analyses the systems used, in order to improve work activities and control resources.

Some or all of these Activities may provide the basis of evidence for your S/NVQ portfolio. All portfolio activities and the Work-based assignment are sign posted with this icon.

The icon states the unit to which the portfolio activities and Work-based assignment relate.

The Work-based assignment, on page 104 suggests that you speak to your manager, finance director or to your colleagues in the accounts office about the way in which budgets are used in your organization. You might like to start thinking now about who to approach and arrange to speak with them.

Session A
Measuring performance

1 Introduction

In many organizations, the only aspect of work that is measured is money – how well is the organization performing against its budgets?

In this session we'll be taking a wider perspective, because budgets are not the only yardstick for measurement, and because first line managers are not the only people with a stake in the way an organization performs. So in this session we'll look at:

- a wide range of methods for measuring performance;
- how an organization's performance might be judged by the various people who have a stake in it.

2 What is performance measurement?

Suppose you run a 100-metre race in 15 seconds. How did you perform? There are lots of ways you could describe it (and you might be tempted to use the way that makes you look best when describing it to other people).

1   You could compare this performance to your previous attempts to run 100 metres. Were you faster or slower?

2   You could compare it to a target you have set for yourself, such as 100 metres in 12 seconds.

3   You could compare it to the times of other people in the race, or (if you are very ambitious!) to the world record time for running 100 metres.

All these descriptions are measurements of your performance. So let's have a definition.

Performance measurement considers how well something performs compared with how it performed in the past, or with how it is required to perform in the future, or in comparison with the performance of something else.

3 Performance measurement principles

In the 100-metre race we said you 'performed it' in 15 seconds, and 15 seconds is a sort of performance measurement. If you usually manage to run 100 metres in 13 seconds we might have said that your performance was 'below average'. If one person beat you in the race we could have said that you came 'second out of eight runners'.

'Below average' and 'second out of eight' are both performance measures.

Activity 1

4 mins

For each of the three measures we used for your 100-metre race, what were you comparing your performance against? Which do you think is the most useful measure?

_____

_____

_____

_____

The first measurement is against the clock: it compares distance travelled with time taken. This is only useful if you happen to know other information, like how long it usually takes people of your age, sex and fitness to run 100 metres. The second is against your own previous performance, and that is useful information for you personally and for people who may compete against you in the near future. The third measurement compares you with other people.

Since I don't know anything else about you, I would say that the third measure is the most useful piece of information you could give me – but I would probably ask you who you were competing against.

The point is, the same performance can be presented in lots of different ways.

Activity 2

3 mins

Say you had to report your performance in the 100-metre race to your coach, your colleagues at work and your partner. Which measure would you use for each person?

1   Your coach _____

2   Your colleagues at work _____

3   Your partner _____

Probably it should be presented in the way that is most helpful to the person who wants the information, but very often information is presented in a way that makes the person presenting it look good.

3.1 Quantitative and qualitative measures

Information is quantitative if it can be expressed in numbers (or 'quantities'). 'Five apples' or '2 kg of apples' or 'a bag of apples costing £1.50' are all examples of quantitative information.

Information is qualitative if it is not expressed in numerical terms (for instance 'below average'), either because it can't be, or because it can't be in a way that has an agreed meaning.

Activity 3 · 3 mins

Describe 'very delicious apples' as fully as you can.

_____

_____

_____

_____

If you need to describe the quality of something, it's generally more helpful to give as much detail as possible. This at least gives someone a chance to judge the apples in comparison to things they know about.

You may argue that 'very delicious apples' could be expressed numerically. You could say 'apples to which I would give a deliciousness rating of 10 out of 10'. But different people have very different ideas about what they think is a delicious apple. How do you judge?

Activity 4 · 3 mins

If you had to choose between the two performance measures for apples below, which would you choose and why?

1　These apples are green, crisp, hard, juicy and sharp on the tongue.

2　I give these apples a deliciousness rating of 5 out of 10, and so do my three colleagues.

_____

_____

_____

I hope you agree that quantitative information (description 2) is the most useful for performance measurement. (This does not mean that qualitative information should never be used, especially if there is a way to express it in a mixture of quantitative (objective) terms and qualitative (subjective) terms.)

If you had bought that bag of apples that rated 5 out of 10, and you wanted to increase your colleagues' apple-eating pleasure, the numbers give you a very clear target to beat: you just have to shop around for apples that rate more highly.

In addition, by saying '… and so do my three colleagues', the second measure is much more convincing than the first, purely personal opinion.

Activity 5 · 3 mins

In a supermarket you notice that the label on one of the bottles of organic apple juice you are thinking of buying has 'Silver Award Winner' printed on it. Is this an example of performance measurement? If so, why?

Look back at the definition of performance measurement at the beginning of this session if you are not sure.

_____

_____

_____

The award implies that the apple juice performed well enough to come second overall in an organic apple juice competition (presumably judged by experts) in comparison with other juices, so yes it is certainly a performance measure.

Watch out for other examples of attempts to 'quantify' qualitative measures. It is a common technique in advertising.

3.2 Comparing numbers: percentages

In this workbook we've already compared actual performance with budgeted performance, by subtracting one number from the other and calling the difference a variance.

There are other ways of looking at numbers in organizations. The most common way in performance measurement is the percentage.

Activity 6

5 mins

Jumbo Ltd manufactures pet products. It had sales of £23,500 in January, £19,900 in February and £27,400 in March. By how much did sales fall in February and rise in March? Express your answer as a percentage to two decimal places.

_____

_____

_____

_____

In February, sales fell by £(23,500 − 19,900) = £3,600. To express this as a percentage, you divide the difference between the two numbers by the earliest number, and multiply by 100: £(3,600/23,500) × 100% = 15.32%.

In March sales rose (compared with February, the earliest number) by £(27,400 − 19,900) = £7,500, or £7,500/£19,900 × 100% = 37.69%.

Another way of looking at this is simply to divide one number by the other. For instance you could say that February sales are only 84.68% (£19,900/£23,500) of January sales, while March saw sales of 137.69% of February sales. (Remember: it is the thing that the percentage is 'of' that represents 100%.)

	£	%		£	%
February	19,900	84.68	**February**	19,900	**100.00**
Decrease	3,600	15.32	Increase	7,500	37.69
January	23,500	**100.00**	March	27,400	137.69

Here are a few examples of how percentages are used in performance measurement.

■ **Market share**
A company may set a target of 25% share of the total market for its product. The marketing department's performance will be measured on the difference between this and the actual market share achieved.

■ **Capacity levels**
'The factory is working at 15% below full capacity' is an example suggesting that the factory is not producing as much as it could, perhaps because of inefficiencies.

■ **Staff turnover**
If a department has staff turnover of 15% over a year, when the average in the organization is only 5%, there may be some problem in the way that department is performing.

3.3 Comparing like with like

Activity 7

5 mins

We have the following additional information about Jumbo Ltd.

Sales	2003	2004
January	23,500	34,200
February	19,900	28,900
March	27,400	48,200

Can you see a pattern here? Describe them below, as fully as you can. What reasons can you think of for the pattern?

_____

_____

_____

_____

_____

_____

You should be able to see a pattern: sales fall in February and rise in March in both years. There could be a number of reasons for this: perhaps the January figures are boosted by post-Christmas sales, February is about normal and March is the time when the company releases its new Spring range of products.

In a case like this, it is not particularly useful to compare a month with the month before, since we already know roughly how sales will rise and fall between January and March. It is not really fair to compare March sales (the new product range) with February sales (the end of the old product range): we are not comparing like with like.

A better way of measuring would be to compare sales in 2004 with sales in 2003.

Sales	2003	2004	Increase
January	23,500	34,200	45.53%
February	19,900	28,900	45.23%
March	27,400	48,200	75.91%

Here we can see that in both January and February, sales are about 45% higher than they were in the previous year. But in March, sales are 75% higher than last year: the Spring 2004 product range has been much more successful on its launch than the Spring 2003 range was when it was first introduced.

If you get unexpected results you should always check that the principle of comparing like with like is being applied.

Just think of the 100-metre race: if all the other competitors were 30 years older than you, your work colleagues might not be quite so impressed that you came second!

Activity 8 · 4 mins

Company A made a profit in the year to 31 December 2003 of £73,900. In the same period, Company B made a profit of £82,500.

What other information would you need to compare the performance of these two companies?

_____

_____

_____

_____

_____

_____

On the face of it, Company B did a bit better than Company A, but we have no idea whether we are comparing like with like.

If Company A's sales were £100,000 and Company B's sales were £500,000, then Company A was actually a lot more successful. We can see this by calculating the profit margin – profit divided by sales – and comparing these.

	Profit (£)	Sales (£)	Profit margin
Company A	73,900	100,000	73.9%
Company B	82,500	500,000	16.5%

It would also be useful to know what the two companies actually do. Company A might be a firm of solicitors while Company B might make bathroom accessories, in which case there is little point in comparing their performance.

More information about costs would be helpful. Perhaps Company B had unusually large expenses during the year that will not recur in subsequent years.

And it would be helpful to know how much profit the companies made in previous years.

4 A range of performance measures

In most business organizations, popular ways of measuring performance are profitability, activity and productivity.

■ **Profitability**
Profit is income less costs. All parts of an organization incur costs, and so everyone's performance can be judged in relation to cost. Only some parts of an organization receive income, and their success should be judged in terms of both cost and income.

- **Activity**

  All parts of an organization carry out activities. An example of an activity measure is 'Number of orders received from customers'. This is a measure of the effectiveness of the marketing department. Activities can be measured in terms of physical numbers, monetary value, or time spent.

- **Productivity**

  This is the quantity of the product or service produced in relation to the resources put in, for example so many units produced per hour, or per employee, or per tonne of material. These are measures of efficiency.

Activity 9

2 mins

Circuit Ltd makes circuit boards for the electronics industry. Its production department has two production targets. Identify which is an activity target, and which is a productivity target.

1   At least 15 batches of circuit boards should be produced each week.

      Activity target ❐   **Productivity target** ❐

2   At least 1,000 circuit boards should be produced per hour of production time.

      Activity target ❐   **Productivity target** ❐

Circuit Ltd produces circuit boards in batches, and in one week it can produce at least 15 batches. We don't know how many boards there are in each batch, nor how many resources are used in a week, so Target 1 is an activity target. Target 2 measures both factory time and the number of circuit boards produced, so this is a productivity target.

5 Financial performance measures

Financial measures are calculated using figures in the organization's accounting records. Financial measures only tell us something about whether performance is good or bad because they are **compared** with something else.

Activity 10 · 4 mins

Here are some examples of financial performance measures, accompanied by comments that you might typically read in the financial pages of a newspaper (these are derived from the *Financial Times*).

For each one, try to identify what the performance is being compared with, and what the comparison shows.

■ Profit: 'the company made pre-tax profits in 2002 of £1.46 m (2001: £1 m) on sales of £12.7 m (2001: £10.7 m)'.

_____

■ Sales: 'the aluminium division had sales which accounted for approximately 10% of the group's total sales'.

_____

■ Costs: 'savings from the cost-reduction programme were £30 m a quarter'.

_____

■ Share price: 'the group's share price rose 15p to 684p despite the stock market's overall fall'.

_____

You may have expressed your ideas differently but see how they compare with mine.

■ This year's profits and sales are compared with last year's, and are found to be higher.
■ Sales for one part of the organization are compared with the total for the group. The comparison shows a certain level of sales, but does not indicate whether this is an improvement or a deterioration.
■ Costs are compared with a previous period. They are at a lower level, in keeping with a planned reduction.
■ Share price is higher than before and high relative to the performance of the stock market as a whole.

Here is a list of yard-sticks against which figures in an organization's accounts are usually placed so that they become measures.

■ Budgeted sales, costs and profits, or standards in a standard costing system.
■ The trend over time (comparing last year to this year, say).

- The results of other departments of the organization.
- The results of other organizations, especially competitors.
- The market in general.
- The economy in general.
- The organization's future potential (for example a promising new organization may make large losses in its first few years, but its performance should be judged in terms of how long it will be before it starts to make large profits).

Activity 11

10 mins

See if you can get hold of a copy of your own organization's latest Annual Report and Accounts and glance through it to see what sort of financial performance measures you can spot.

_____

_____

_____

_____

_____

If you've studied any accounting you'll know that there are several ratios that can be calculated to show how an organization is performing. Examples are the current ratio, profit margin and return on capital employed. Another workbook in this series, _Understanding Organizations in their Context_, tells you about financial ratios in more detail.

I logged on to the Internet and tapped 'Annual Report and Accounts' into a search engine.

The first thing I found was the Annual Report and Accounts of Unilever, which has a liberal sprinkling of financial performance measures just in the first few pages. Examples I found were: 'Leading brands account for 84% of total sales …', 'In Africa, Middle East and Turkey, overall sales were up by 2%, with profits increasing by 13%' and many others.

6 Non-financial performance measures

Financial measures do not necessarily give the full picture of an organization's performance, and in any case as a first line manager you may not have access to many accounting figures for your section or department.

Activity 12

3 mins

What measures would you prefer to see for judging your work team's performance? Does the accounting system measure these?

_____

_____

_____

_____

_____

Your team may be best judged by looking at units produced, time taken, product quality, delivery, after-sales service or customer satisfaction, none of which is directly measured by the traditional accounting system.

Unlike traditional variance reports, non-financial indicators are more relevant for non-financial managers, who can understand and therefore use them more effectively.

We can supplement financial measures in each of the following key areas of an organization:

- sales-related activities;
- materials;
- labour.

6.1 Sales-related activities

Traditionally, sales performance is measured in terms of price and volume variances, but other possible measures include revenue targets and target market share. You can analyse these measures in as much detail as you like: by country or by region, by individual products, by salesperson and so on.

Example of a financial measure.

- _Sales are up by 14%._

Examples of non-financial measures.

- **Goods returned: total sales**
  '0.5% of goods were returned by customers.'

This helps you to monitor customer satisfaction, and is a check on whether quality control procedures are working

- **Deliveries late: deliveries on schedule**
  '12% late deliveries.'
  This comparison can be applied both to sales made to customers and to receipts from suppliers, and measures the efficiency of the stores department

- **Number of people served and speed of service**
  '100 people served in one hour.'
  In a shop, if it takes too long to reach the checkout point, customers will go elsewhere and future sales will be lost.

- **Customer profitability analysis**
  'An average of £100 profit was made per customer.'
  This measure may not be so useful, as profitability can vary widely between different customers. Different customers may be given different levels of discount, delivery costs are higher the further away the customer is, some customers demand more support than others, and so on. Information on this can help you check whether individual customers are actually profitable to sell to, and whether profitability can be improved for any customer by switching effort from one type of activity to another.

Activity 13

5 mins

A motor insurance company has collected the following data about claims on its insurance policies in the last year.

Age group	Number of policies	Total premiums (£)	Total claims (£)	Profit or loss (£)
18–25	2,700	837,000	855,000	
25–35	3,400	1,003,000	520,000	
35–50	5,400	1,350,000	120,000	
50–65	3,400	765,000	20,000	
Over 65	1,000	305,000	300,000	

Which group of customers is the most profitable for the insurance company and which is the least profitable?

Subtract the total claims from the total premiums per group to give you the profit per group. (You can also divide the profit per group by the number of policies to find out the average profit per person.)

	Total premiums (£)	Total claims (£)	Profit or loss (£)	Profit or loss per policy (£)
18–25	837,000	855,000	−18,000	−6.67
25–35	1,003,000	520,000	483,000	142.06
35–50	1,350,000	120,000	1,230,000	227.78
50–65	765,000	20,000	745,000	219.18
Over 65	305,000	300,000	5,000	5.00

The 18 to 25 age group is the only one that is not profitable, and the 35 to 50 age group is most profitable.

You might think that the company should stop selling insurance policies to 18 to 25 year olds – but they will of course get older and become more responsible drivers. The company will want to keep them as customers in the future.

What about the tiny profit made on policies sold to those aged over 65? This is probably a lot of work for little income, and the company might consider either raising the premiums or stop selling insurance to people over 65.

6.2 Materials

Traditional measures for materials are standard costs, and price and usage variances. Again there are many non-financial measures that can be helpful.

- **General physical quality**
  This will be important to the final product. Materials may have to have smoothness, or hardness, or pliability, or consistency of colour or taste.
- **Particular physical quality**
  The material may need to be perfectly round or weigh a specific amount. Nothing less than 100% performance will do.

Activity 14

4 mins

You are a first line production manager working in a perfume bottling factory. You are responsible for manufacturing the stoppers for the tops of the bottles, and your colleague is responsible for ensuring that the perfume is not contaminated by other smells as it is bottled.

What non-financial performance measures could you expect to see for each process?

_____

_____

_____

_____

_____

_____

_____

Measures in such cases can be expressed in terms of number of defects: '2 out of every 100 stoppers produced had the hole in the wrong position'; '6 out of every 10,000 bottles of perfume failed the "sniffer" test'.

The performance of materials suppliers should also be measured: how quickly they deliver materials, whether they are ever late with their deliveries, and how many of the items they deliver are sent back because they are faulty.

6.3 Labour

Labour costs are traditionally measured in terms of rate and volume variances.

Other staff-related measures are possible, such as:

- unit sales per salesperson;
- time taken to do a task;
- hours lost through sickness.

Almost any aspect of an organization can be measured in terms of the different individuals or teams who carry out activities.

Qualitative measures concentrate on things like:

- ability to communicate;
- relationships with colleagues;
- customers' impressions ('so and so was extremely helpful/rude');
- levels of skills attained.

Employee-based measures are very important when assessing the perform-ance of the employees' manager, as well as the employee. High profitability or tight cost control should not be accompanied by 100% staff turnover!

Activity 15

5 mins

John works in the Claims Processing Department of an insurance company with 14 colleagues. They are all paid £18,200 per annum and work a 7-hour day, 5 days a week. The department typically handles 1,500 claims each week of the year.

The department's manager wants to measure the performance of the depart-ment. Identify as many useful performance measures as you can think of, explaining what each is intended to measure and how it is calculated.

_____

_____

_____

_____

One morning John spends half an hour on the phone to his sister, who lives in Australia, at the company's expense. The cost of the call proves to be £16. What is the cost of John's half hour of idle time?

_____

_____

Here are some suggestions for measures, with explanations of how they are calculated.

- Claims processed per employee per week: 1,500/15 = 100 (activity measure).
- Staff cost per claim: (£18,200 × 15)/(1,500 × 52) = £3.50 (profitability measure).
- Claims processed per department hour: 1,500/(7 × 5) = 42.9 (productivity measure).
- Cost of John's half hour of idle time: £16 + £5 = £21 (profitability measure). John earns £10 per hour: £18,200/(7 × 5 × 52) or £5 per half hour.

You may have thought of other measures and probably have slight rounding differences.

6.4 Dangers of non-financial measures

If you have too many measures you will be overloaded with information and may not be able to act on any of it properly.

Non-financial measures might lead managers to pursue detailed goals for their own departments, and lose sight of the goals for the organization as a whole.

7 External comparisons

Suppose you read in the newspaper that 'X plc made a profit of £3 m, as opposed to £7 m last year'.

On the face of it, it looks as if X plc has not done very well this year. But you should be well aware by now that it is not fair to pass judgement without comparing X plc's performance with something else.

7.1 The state of the economy

Economic influences should be considered whenever an organization's performance is measured.

Activity 16

What factors in the economy as a whole would you consider if you were assessing the performance of X plc, a retailer?

_____

_____

_____

_____

You may have questioned whether the economy is booming or in recession. Is the government trying to encourage organization growth, control inflation, reduce unemployment, or balance imports and exports?

Economic factors like these will affect interest rates and taxation, foreign exchange rates, the availability of skilled staff, and – crucially for X plc – the willingness of customers to spend money. All these things will have an impact on X plc's performance.

7.2 Competitors

You can compare the performances of different business organizations by calculating the same financial measures for each one, using published accounts, to see whose are better and whose are worse than average.

You can also get information about competitors through:

- newspaper and magazine reports and articles;
- their promotional material, advertising, website and so on;
- market research;
- recruiting ex-employees of rival organizations.

Activity 17 · · 8 mins

Find out the following economic figures. You could look in a broadsheet newspaper such as *The Times*, or search the Internet (for instance, http://www.statistics.gov.uk/ is a good source).

Rate of inflation _____   Bank base lending rate _____

Exchange rates: pound sterling/US dollar _____ pound sterling/euro _____

Rates of corporation tax _____

We won't give answers, because all these figures are likely to have changed by the time you read this. Hopefully, in the course of your research you will also come across other economic statistics that are relevant to your own organization's industry.

7.3 Benchmarking

Benchmarking analyses the performance of your own organization, or part of it, compared with the performance of another organization or part, which is generally regarded as 'the best' at the activity in question.

There are several types of benchmarking.

- **Competitor benchmarking** looks at direct competitors using any available published information, plus information from customer and supplier interviews.
- **Process benchmarking** looks at similar 'processes' in different organizations. For example, British Airways learned lessons about how to maintain their aircraft in foreign airports by looking at processes in organizations that maintain photocopiers.
- **Internal benchmarking** looks at different parts of the same organization, such as the security measures taken in different branches of the same shop to see which approach is most effective at preventing shop-lifting.

Activity 18

3 mins

What do you think are the advantages of benchmarking? Can you see any disadvantages?

_____

_____

_____

_____

Benchmarking is a good way of avoiding complacency, and it can give rise to new ideas. Also, staff are more likely to accept that they are not being asked to perform miracles if they can actually see new methods working in another organization.

But you probably spotted that persuading other organizations to share information may be a problem. Direct competitors won't want to give away their secrets or reveal their weaknesses. Worse, they may provide false information.

And processes can't always be transferred successfully. A way of working that succeeds in one organization may not work at all in another organization, especially if it depends on the talents of particular individuals.

8 Stakeholders and their objectives

Different people are interested in different aspects of performance, so it is measured in lots of different ways. For every organization there are individuals, groups of people, and other organizations, each of whom has an interest (a 'stake') in how the organization performs.

These people are called **stakeholders**, and there are three main types:

- **Internal stakeholders**: employees, at all levels.
- **Connected stakeholders:** owners; shareholders; members or subscribers of the organization; customers; financiers (banks, venture capitalists and the like); suppliers and partners.
- **External stakeholders**: the general community, local and central government, pressure groups and professional or industry bodies.

Activity 19

Who else might have an interest (or a 'stake') in your performance in the 100-metre race?

_____

_____

_____

If I ran in this race I have to admit that my doctor would probably be rather concerned, and would be standing by with a resuscitator! Hopefully you had lots of better ideas.

- Other people in your race would be interested, and competitors in other heats.
- Your team-mates taking part in other events would want you to win points for the team.
- The race officials would be concerned that the race was conducted fairly.
- The audience would probably have favourites: they may even have placed bets on how well you will do.

8.1 Internal stakeholders

Everyone who works for the organization, from the most junior new recruit to the senior managers, is an internal stakeholder.

They have a personal stake in the organization's continued existence, because it is a place where they spend a great deal of their time and energy, and it pays their wages or salaries.

Employees also have more specific individual interests and goals. Here are some typical examples:

- A secure income, and probably increases in income over time.
- Career development.
- Human contact and a sense of belonging to a team.
- Interesting work that offers opportunities to use and develop skills.
- A safe and pleasant working environment.
- A sense of doing something worthwhile.

Activity 20

3 mins

Suppose your organization has announced that it is about to make some staff redundant, and jobs in your department are at risk. How might individuals' personal objectives affect their performance and so the overall performance of the department?

_____

_____

_____

_____

I would say the answer depends on what each person's main objectives are, whether they like their job, what their other prospects are, and what they stand to gain or lose from being made redundant.

Staff members who don't like their job much may well let their performance drop off. And if they stand to receive a generous enough redundancy package to leave them financially secure until they find another job, they won't make any special effort for the organization.

Staff whose prospects elsewhere are bad, or who are very keen to stay on because of personal objectives will probably perform extra well, to make it clear to managers that they are indispensable.

8.2 Connected stakeholders

Connected stakeholders include the following:

■ **Owners, shareholders, members or subscribers**
Their objective is to get a return on the money (or time, if it is a club) they have invested in the organization. If they did not invest their money, the organization would not exist at all, so earning a return is usually a commercial organization's prime objective.

■ **Customers**
They want products and services that meet their needs. They are interested in quality, price and dependability of supply. Customers can be very powerful (for instance, Sainsbury's is a much bigger organization than most of the ones it buys from) and have a huge effect on prices and procedures. Individual customers may band together into user groups with a strong interest in performance. Customers of rail and bus services are good examples.

■ **Financiers**
They want to know that any loan or overdraft they make, and the interest on it, will be repaid.

■ **Suppliers and partners**
They expect to be paid, so they have a stake in the organization's financial stability. They will also be keen to do future business, so it is in their interests that the organization survives and grows.

Activity 21

3 mins

Suppliers are sometimes regarded as 'the enemy'. Purchasing departments seek out the lowest-price suppliers and constantly switch supply sources to avoid getting too dependent on any individual supplier. Supplier contracts feature heavy penalty clauses and are drawn up in a spirit of general mistrust of all external providers. Information is deliberately withheld in case the supplier uses it to gain power during price negotiations.

What are the disadvantages of treating suppliers in this way?

_____

_____

_____

_____

_____

If you always pay late, or disrupt suppliers' plans by placing impossible demands upon them, or switch contracts, eventually no supplier will want to do business with you.

But there is a bigger disadvantage: the supplier's knowledge and skills are not exploited effectively. You buy products and services from suppliers because they are better at providing them than you are. The more they know about your product, your customers' needs, and your plans for the future, the better able they will be to provide you with the supplies you need.

Forward-thinking organizations recognize this and enter into partnerships with key suppliers. They open up their design departments and share their supply problems, and this helps generate new ideas, solutions, and products.

It may well be in your interest to share information with suppliers. This applies within organizations, too: if your work team is dependent on another to supply materials or information, it is in your interest to collaborate with the other work team as much as possible.

8.3 External stakeholders

External stakeholders are varied and have very varied objectives. Here are some examples.

- **The general community**
  This is interested because organizations bring local employment and facilities (shops, restaurants), and national benefits such as exports and know-how. They can also affect the natural environment, for instance by increasing road traffic, polluting water or air, or making excessive noise.
- **Local and central government**
  They are interested in tax revenue, compliance with laws that are meant to benefit everyone, such as the Health and Safety at Work Act, and employment prospects.
- **Pressure groups**
  They have particular interest in certain aspects of the organization's activities. For example, animal rights activists may object to an organization's methods of testing products.
- **Professional or industry bodies**
  They seek to develop 'best practice' standards and defend their members' interests where there is possible conflict with other external stakeholders. They also ensure that members' activities don't bring the profession or industry into disrepute.

Activity 22

What aspects of your organization's performance would a trade union be interested in?

_____

_____

_____

_____

_____

_____

You may have some ideas that are specific to your organization, but here are some general suggestions.

- Rates of pay, and pay rises, relative to other equivalent organizations.
- Statistics about recruitment policy, particularly with regard to ethnic and minority groups.
- Workers' rights and working conditions.
- Output and productivity information, since this is relevant to job security and the fairness of rates of pay.

8.4 Differing objectives

The objectives of all these different stakeholders can be sharply in conflict.

Activity 23

Company A has made a large profit in the last financial year, and its shareholders and bank are very pleased. Why might the stakeholders below be less satisfied?

Internal stakeholders

_____

_____

Customers

_____

_____

The community

_____

_____

Suppliers

_____

_____

In a situation like this you have to put yourself in the shoes of the other stakeholders. How did the company make its profits?

■ It might pay very low wages or expect staff to work impossibly long hours.
■ Corners might have been cut, with an adverse effect on the quality of the product.
■ No money may have been spent on local community projects.
■ No money may have been spent developing innovative new products.

I hope you can see that different information is useful depending on what your stake in the organization is and what you want to know about it.

Many organizations have developed performance measurement systems to report on a variety of aspects of performance and reflect the interests of all stakeholders. Let's look at one of the best-known modern approaches, the balanced scorecard.

8.5 The balanced scorecard

This looks at an organization from four different points of view.

Perspective	Question	Areas of concern and examples of performance targets
Customer	What do existing and new customers value from us?	Cost, quality, delivery etc. 'Deliver within two working days'
Internal	What processes must we excel at to achieve our financial and customer objectives?	Internal ways of doing things and decision making 'Minimize stock holding costs'
Innovation and learning	Can we continue to improve and create future value?	Ability to acquire new skills and develop new products 'Sales of new products to be 20% of sales of existing ones' 'Minimize time to market for new products' 'Increase spend on training by 10%'
Financial	How do we create value for our shareholders?	Ability to increase return to shareholders 'Widen profit margins by 2%'

EXTENSION 1
If you want to find out more about implementing this very useful technique, try following the guidance in *Balanced Scorecard Step-by-Step: Maximizing Performance and Maintaining Results* by P. R. Niven and R. S. Kaplan.

You can see that answers to the questions help identify areas for improvement. Appropriate performance targets (both financial and non-financial) can then be set.

For instance if the answer to the question 'What do customers value?' is 'fast delivery', then specific targets can be set ('Deliver within two working days'). Internal processes that aim to ensure delivery in two days can be set up, and performance can be monitored to see whether the target is being met.

A 'process' is simply a way of doing something. If you run out of a certain raw material, for example, there will be a 'process' for getting new supplies, such as: 'Write out a stock requisition, get it authorized by the project manager, send it to the purchasing department, identify the best supplier, place an order, take delivery and check for quality, accept delivery into stores'. The target might be to maintain a minimum level of stock and to avoid going out of stock of any item.

The scorecard is balanced because managers are expected to take account of all four perspectives when they look at performance. This should prevent improvements being made in one area at the expense of others.

Activity 24

A company develops a new car with indicators that get louder as the car goes faster, so that they are not accidentally left flashing when driving at high speed on a motorway. The company has the processes and technology to make such a device at a reasonable cost.

Use the balanced scorecard to see whether this is a good idea.

Perspective	Question	Evaluation
Customer	What do existing and new customers value from us?	
Internal	What processes must we excel at to achieve our financial and customer objectives?	
Innovation and learning	Can we continue to improve and create future value?	
Financial	How do we create value for our shareholders?	

At first this sounds like a good innovation in response to a specific customer need. Certainly the evaluation of the internal, innovation/learning and financial perspectives would be positive.

But if you think about it a little more deeply, it may be that the customer perspective is wrong – that what the customer really wants is a better sound-proofed car with a quieter engine, not an even noisier car!

This is an example of focusing too much on innovation without thinking through what the customer really values.

Activity 25

S/NVQ D6

This activity may provide the basis of appropriate evidence for your S/NVQ portfolio. If you are intending to take this course of action it might be better to write your answers on separate sheets of paper.

Draw up a balanced scorecard for your part of your organization, and aim to include at least three performance measures under each heading.

You will need to begin by identifying the stakeholders in your part of the organization and determining what their interests are. Remember that other departments are 'customers' of your department, and your department has its own internal suppliers.

The financial perspective can include budget targets if this is most appropriate.

Looking at the completed scorecard, what ideas for improvements does it suggest?

Self-assessment 1

20 mins

1 Here is some performance information for two factories owned by the same organization. They both make Product X. The figures show the numbers of units of Product X produced by each factory. Your task is to produce a numerical comparison of the performance of the two factories, and comment on what you find.

	Quarter 1	**Quarter 2**	**Quarter 3**	**Quarter 4**
Factory A	31,200	31,000	34,300	29,800
Factory B	18,500	19,300	16,200	31,700

_____

_____

_____

_____

_____

_____

_____

2 What measures could you devise to assess staff morale amongst your work team? Try to think of three. Remember that quantitative measures are more useful than qualitative measures.

_____

_____

_____

_____

_____

_____

_____

3   Fill in the missing words in the following sentences.

■ Benchmarking is a good way of avoiding _____ and it may give rise to _____ _____.

■ The main interest of shareholders is to get a _____ on their _____, so _____ is usually thought of as a commercial organization's prime objective.

■ The balanced scorecard looks at an organization from four different points of view.

a _____

b _____

c _____

d _____

Answers to these questions can be found on pages 116–17.

9 Summary

- Performance measurement looks at how well something performs compared with how it performed in the past, or how it is required to perform in the future, or how something else performs.

- Quantitative information is most useful because it gives you a clear target to beat.

- It is important to make sure that you are comparing like with like.

- An organization's performance is judged on profitability, productivity and activity.

- Financial performance indicators compare performance against budget, the trend over time, other organizations, the economy in general and future potential.

- Non-financial measures look at specific aspects, such as the number of people served or the time taken to do something.

- External comparisons can be made against the general economy and competitors, and by benchmarking against competitors, other processes or other internal departments.

- Stakeholders are internal (employees), connected (owners, customers, financiers, suppliers), and external (community, government, pressure groups, professional bodies). Their objectives may be in conflict.

- The balanced scorecard is a performance measurement framework that takes account of the interests of all stakeholders.

Session B
Monitoring and improving performance

1 Introduction

In this session we are going to see how you could actually set up a performance management system for your own department, and what you might do with it once it was in place.

Here's an outline of a series of steps to follow in establishing and operating your own system.

■ **Set performance standards**
Decide what you need to measure the performance of, then define what is meant by 'performance', and what is 'acceptable performance'.

■ **Monitor performance**
Devise ways of measuring performance that show you whether or not you are performing to the standard expected. Create a system to collect the information you'll need to calculate the measures, and then put it into practice: collect the information and calculate the measures on a regular basis. Finally, report them to the people who need to know.

■ **Improve performance**
Following performance reports, take appropriate action so that you maintain, and hopefully improve, performance in the future.

2 Developing performance standards

A performance 'standard' is a performance measure that says a particular level of performance should be achieved.

If you heard something described simply as 'standard' you would expect it to be no better or worse than another, acceptable example of the same thing. If you heard about 'high standards', you would expect something better than what is usually expected.

Setting performance standards is a three-part process.

- Define what it is you are measuring.
- Find out what is acceptable.
- Establish a level of performance as the standard.

2.1 What are you measuring?

So what 'performance' is it that you will be measuring? To answer this question you first need to consider the purpose of your part of the organization – that is, what it actually performs.

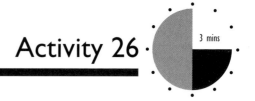

Activity 26   3 mins

What is the purpose of your part of your organization? Avoid the temptation to go into detail: define it as simply as you can.

_____

_____

_____

_____

A short and simple phrase or sentence will do as an answer. Here are some examples I've thought of.

- We assemble the engines that form part of products X, Y and Z.
- We answer general correspondence and deal with telephone calls from customers.
- We create artwork and computer graphics for company publications.
- We process claims on household contents insurance policies.

2.2 What is 'acceptable' performance?

We saw earlier that performance means different things to different people.

Activity 27 · 4 mins

Who are your work team's particular stakeholders?

_____

_____

What aspects of your work team's performance matter to them?

_____

_____

_____

Here are some possible stakeholders for an individual work team that I have thought of. Perhaps you came up with the same ones?

- **Customers**
  Even if you do not deal directly with the people who buy your organization's products and services, you still have customers in the sense that someone (an internal customer) uses the output of your department in the next stage of the process.

  Whether they are internal or external, customers are concerned that your output should be delivered when they need it, and be free of faults. That is their standard for you.

■ **Senior managers**
They expect to see your department comply with the organization's rules and policies, such as hours of work ('all staff will work from 9 to 5 and take one hour for lunch between 12 am and 2 pm').

■ **External stakeholders**
They may be involved, for instance if your work requires you to follow certain rules and procedures prescribed by the government. A payroll department is a good example: they have to follow rules and meet deadlines set by the Inland Revenue, to the letter.

■ **Your colleagues and you yourself**
You are all internal stakeholders, of course, and you will be concerned about matters such as levels of pay, how enjoyable and absorbing the work is, opportunities for career progression, and so on.

Individuals have different standards for these things.

2.3 Setting standards

Armed with as much information as you can glean from stakeholders, you can now begin to set standards.

Wherever you can, quantify the information. For instance, if customers expect 'fast' delivery but don't specify what they mean by 'fast', you can find out how quickly your department delivers on average.

You then have a choice of whether to use that average, based on current working conditions, as the initial standard, or whether to be more ambitious.

■ Attainable (or 'expected') standards are based on the premise that work will be carried out efficiently, equipment will be properly operated and materials will be properly used. An allowance can be made for inefficiencies if there is no way of avoiding them, given current working conditions.

■ Ideal standards are based on perfect operating conditions: no inefficiencies, no lost or wasted time, no machine breakdowns or computer crashes, no wasted or spoiled materials.

We'll come back to this choice later. For now, assume that we have decided to be realistic and set standards that we know are attainable.

Activity 28

A call centre has the following information about how long 10 examples of a particular type of customer query took to be resolved during a period of one week.

Call	Minutes
1	1
2	5
3	6
4	7
5	9
6	6
7	8
8	5
9	6
10	7

The call centre has set a performance standard that says that 95% of all such queries should be resolved within the standard time set, which is six minutes.

_____

How many times did the call centre meet the standard (i.e. the query took the standard time or less to be resolved).

_____

Did the company meet its standard during the week in question?

_____

Unfortunately only six out of the ten calls were completed within the standard time. This is 6/10 × 100% = 60% of calls, so the company is failing to achieve its standard of 95% by a long way.

3 Monitoring performance

In theory you could monitor performance simply by asking your stakeholders now and then to tell you what they think, but this does not give you much control over what is going on.

A much better approach is to record relevant activities of your department as they happen, and then analyse and review the performance measures on a regular basis.

The issue of collecting information and analysing it is covered in depth in other workbooks in this series: *Obtaining Information for Effective Management* and *Solving Problems and Making Decisions.*

Computers or computerized machines can collect a mass of data about how much time and other resources are used on any task. But to analyse such data requires your time and effort.

Indeed, the cost of collecting the information required to produce a performance should be carefully weighed up against the benefits of having that particular measure.

3.1 Measuring performance against standards

Let's say your customers expect fast delivery of your department's output, and you have calculated that **on average** it takes two days for your work team to produce the output. You are thinking about using this as the standard.

It is only an **average** figure, so sometimes it must take longer than two days, and sometimes it must take less. Really, it would be better if the performance standard was: '**guaranteed** delivery within **no more than** two days', but to achieve this, the work of your department probably needs to be analysed in more detail.

You need to identify all the processes and inputs involved in performing tasks, and the relationships between them; you need to find out what is normal; and then you need to use measures to see where failures and errors occur.

This may not be information that you calculate on a regular basis, but information that you **could** calculate if there has been some variance from expected performance, and you need to interpret the numbers and investigate the cause.

The measures you might calculate to do this for a particular area of performance will often combine and compare measures from the chart shown below.

Common measures of areas of performance	
Area of performance	**Common measures**
Error or failure	Absenteeism/sickness rates Complaints received Defects detected Incidents of equipment failure Time spent waiting or time late Miscalculations made Misinformation given Returned goods received Incidents of being out of stock Claims under warranties
Time taken	Measured per second, minute, hour, day, week, month or year Measured per shift or cycle
Quantity produced etc.	Range of products made Number of parts/components held Units produced Units sold Services performed kg/litres/metres of product produced Number of documents produced or processed Deliveries made Enquiries received
People's activities	Number of employees Range of employee skills Number of repeat customers Size of competitors Range of suppliers

You can use this chart in a number of ways to create a very large number of performance measures, simply by inserting the word 'per'.

- Compare items in different columns, for instance 'Absenteeism per employee' or 'Equipment failures per day'.
- Compare items in the same column, for instance litres (of some resource) used per unit produced'. 'Documents produced per service performed' might show you that a particular task seemed to generate an unusually large amount of paperwork: something worth investigating by looking at that task and the associated documents themselves.

You can also combine elements in more elaborate ways: for instance you might be interested to know the number of units sold by a particular employee per month compared with the total number of units sold by all employees in that month.

Activity 29

S/NVQ D6

This activity may provide the basis of appropriate evidence for your S/NVQ portfolio. If you are intending to take this course of action it might be better to write your answers on separate sheets of paper.

The common performance measures chart that we have just seen is not all-inclusive of course, so you need to make it more useful to you in your work.

Adapt some of the common performance measures so that they are relevant to your work team: for 'range of products', for instance, you could substitute specific products made or services provided by your work team. You will need to delete some items as not being relevant.

- Using your personalized chart, devise at least four performance measures that might be useful to help you manage your department.

- Explain why they might be useful.

- Explain how you would collect the information relevant to your performance measures.

Obviously I don't know which measures would be useful in your situation, but here are some suggestions, showing ways of using the chart.

- 'Miscalculations per 1,000 invoices' would show how accurately someone in the Accounts Department was working.
- 'Defects per item returned' may show that poor-quality goods are being sold or (if there are no defects in returned goods) that customers' real needs are not being properly identified.

- 'Misinformation per 100 customer enquiries' may show you how knowledgeable and well-trained your customer service staff are.
- 'Customers waiting per minute' shows you how long the queue in your shop is.

3.2 Being realistic

Of course, one way of dealing with a failure to meet a performance standard is to set a **lower** standard!

Obviously that is not desirable in the long term, but there may be occasions when there is no other option because of matters that are outside your control.

For example, if your department requires a certain number of highly-trained people to operate effectively and there is a sudden flu epidemic, the chances are that you will fail to meet your normal standards for a time.

The best thing to do is to be totally open about it. At the earliest opportunity, tell everyone who relies on your department's performance that you won't meet your targets. Then they have the chance to make alternative arrangements or, if none can be made, to alert their own customers to the fact that things have been held up.

There are other situations in which standards might be revised. For example, the standard time for doing a task using a certain piece of equipment might change when a new version of the equipment is acquired. It would be meaningless to compare current performance using the new equipment with the old standard.

On the other hand, if you change standards too frequently, people might think you are constantly 'moving the goal posts'. Your staff will not be motivated to perform well if they can never reach the standard required. This is the problem with so-called 'ideal standards', mentioned earlier.

I would say that you should adjust standards when changes of a permanent nature occur, but not in response to temporary 'blips'.

3.3 Performance reports

Performance reports should be produced and examined as often as they are needed. Your managers might want to see a report once a week or once a month, because they assume you have everything pretty much under control.

You might want to see a report at the end of each day, or perhaps more often, to make sure that you really do have things under control.

There is no prescribed format for a performance report: it will be different for each organization and each part of the organization.

■ You may be able to call up a detailed list of performance measures on a computer screen and just glance through the latest figures to reassure yourself about specific issues.

■ Your manager is not likely to want to see a report that goes into a great amount of detail, especially about things that have performed as expected, as most generally do. But he or she will be interested in 'exceptions' – the one or two things that went wrong – and you may well be required to add comments explaining why those things went wrong, and what you have done about it.

Activity 30 · 5 mins

Here is an extract from the performance information available about the work of a sales order processing department. There are 12 people in the department and they work a seven-hour day, five days a week, mostly dealing with orders submitted on paper, though they also deal with some telephone orders.

	Expected	Actual
Staff-hours available	420	440
Orders processed	1500	1450
Calls received	120	130
Returns processed	15	10

As a general rule 'exceptions' are only reported to senior managers when the difference from the expected or target figure is more than 5%.

Which of these figures might senior managers be most interested in, and why?

_____

_____

_____

_____

_____

If you calculate the percentages, you'll find that calls received ($(130-120)/120 \times 100\% = 8.3\%$ more) and returns processed ($(15-10)/15 \times 100\% = 75\%$ less) were both outside the limit. On the other hand, there was not an unmanageably large number of extra calls, and it is good news that there were fewer than expected returns (although actually there might have been many, but they did not get processed at all). Also, both are outside the control of the work team being measured, so the manager is unlikely to be greatly interested.

Do you agree that the most unusual thing in this report is that there were about 4% more staff-hours available than there should have been ($12 \times 7 \times 5 = 420$). This means that the department worked some overtime or had some extra help. Why should they need to do so, since it was a pretty average week?

The lesson here is to try to think like your manager would think (or whoever you are reporting to). Don't just follow the rules blindly: take an overview and think about whether the figures make sense when considered in relation to each other.

4 Improving performance

Let's say that you have a complete set of standards which you are monitoring and reporting on. Is this the end of the process?

No, of course we want to improve performance, and some of the processes that we have just gone through will help us to do this.

4.1 Continuous improvement

In modern organizations it is not enough just to perform to the same standard all the time, even if that standard was originally a good one.

- In commercial organizations at least, competition is fierce: if you just stand still, your competitors will come out with a better product and take your share of the market.
- Technology is changing and advancing faster than ever before, creating new opportunities and making old ways of doing things obsolete.
- Customers have learned to expect higher and higher quality.

The emphasis in modern organizations, therefore, is on continuous improvement. This is essentially about reviewing what you do, identifying problems or areas for improvement, planning and implementing the improvements, reviewing the effects of the improvements, identifying further areas for improvement, and so on.

Relating this to the measurement of performance against standards, we can think of it as a cycle with the following six steps.

1   Set standards and formulate performance measures.

2   Monitor against standards and performance measures (by asking for feedback from stakeholders such as customers and employees, and collecting information relating to performance measures).

3   Identify areas of non-conformance to standards and poor performance, and collect further data.

4   Plan improvements (by identifying possible causes of non-conformance and poor performance and discussing solutions).

5   Implement improvements (in inputs, processes or outputs).

6   Set higher standards and updated performance measures and monitor these (in other words, go back to step 2 again).

Here we will concentrate on step 5 and suggest lots of things that you can either do yourself in your department, or recommend to more senior managers, to make a contribution to the continuous improvement of your organization.

We'll think mainly about improving the performance of a small part of an organization that takes inputs from one department and passes its outputs to another part of the organization.

An example would be a department that takes engine parts and components, assembles the engine, and then passes it to a department that connects the engine up to the car body. Another example would be a department that takes applications for credit from a customer services department, checks the credit status of the applicant, and then passes the application on for final approval by a team in head office.

To help us look at different aspects of performance we'll think in terms of a system.

A system is something that takes **inputs** and performs **processes** on those inputs to produce **outputs**. For example, a bread-making system takes flour, yeast and water (inputs), mixes them up, kneads the mixture, makes it rise and bakes it (processes), and produces loaves of bread (outputs).

Any aspect of work can be seen in this way. In fact an organization as a whole can be seen as a system.

4.2 Improving inputs

The inputs of a department are the resources it uses to make outputs. They include materials, machines and office equipment, information, and above all the people you manage.

We'll save the especially complex issue of people for a separate section and confine our comments here to ways you can improve the performance you get out of other inputs.

■ Find better suppliers for inputs, who can deliver better-quality items, or deliver faster, or more consistently on time, or in more convenient quantities, or who offer a better after-sales support service. Price is always an issue, too, of course: it is good to save money, but remember cheaper supplies may be inferior.

■ Don't regard suppliers as 'the enemy': develop closer partnerships with suppliers so that they understand your needs better.

■ If external information is a key input (for example, information about stock markets, or other companies' activities, or the economic climate in another country) you need that information to be the most up-to-date and accurate available, but you don't need to be overwhelmed. You could subscribe to a specialist information service such as Reuters, who will tailor the information they have available to your precise needs.

■ If inputs to your department are outputs from another department, then you are that department's customer, and you are entitled to express your views about the quality of their work. Again, it is better to view the relationship as a partnership, not as a fight. Perhaps there are ways of improving the layout of the forms on which they supply information to you, or perhaps you could share a database with them to make it easier to exchange information. Perhaps they could give you early warning about any delays in delivery.

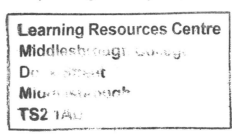

Activity 31

4 mins

You are the manager in charge of the team who operate the checkouts of a medium-sized branch of a supermarket. (It will help if you think about the supermarket you and your family use personally.)

Identify the resources that are the inputs to the checkout process, and recommend at least one way of improving those inputs. (Concentrate on inputs – we'll think about processes and outputs in the next two activities).

_____

_____

_____

_____

_____

_____

These are the checkout inputs in my local supermarket.

■ The people who operate the checkouts, and their time, skill and knowledge.
■ Equipment and 'stationery', including computerized tills and paper till rolls, a conveyor belt, a barcode scanner, a number pad for keying in barcodes that cannot be scanned, a set of electronic scales, a credit card scanner, and a tool for removing security tags from items such as clothing.
■ Information from a system that links up barcodes to product descriptions and prices.
■ The notes and coins in the tills.
■ The supermarket goods chosen by customers (food, toiletries etc.) and plastic bags for them to be carried home.

I think the most obvious ways of improving checkout inputs at my supermarket would be to:

■ have more checkout desks open, which means employing more people;
■ have scanners that work more of the time;
■ have a machine that automates the packing of bags, which I hate, and which holds everyone up.

You might have thought of other improvements to inputs: better training for staff, more barcoded items, a machine that would allow customers to scan in their purchases themselves, or better maintenance and regular cleaning of the conveyor belts – and possibly a host of others, depending what most annoys you about your supermarket!

4.3 Improving processes

There are lots of ways to improve processes. Here are some suggestions.

■ Stop doing unnecessary things just because 'that's the way we've always done it', or 'that's what it says in the procedures manual'.

Although it can be quite a time-consuming exercise, it is worth describing on paper each operation that people in your department perform, and then critically analysing each one. Can you eliminate any activity altogether? Can you combine activities in some way that avoids double-handling? Do you collect information that you never use (I know I do)?

■ Look at your competitors' processes if you can (in other words, benchmark) and simply make sure you start doing things their way if it is better than what you do now. Even if you can't get sufficient competitor information, there may be other departments in your own organization that are worth looking at, especially if your organization has other regional offices or offices overseas.

■ Consider contracting out to external suppliers any processes that don't absolutely have to be done in-house (outsourcing). This allows you to concentrate on what you do best.

■ Change the layout of the work area and storage space to ensure that people who frequently need to work together on a process are physically close to each other and to the things they need to do their jobs.

■ Use computer technology to its full potential, especially to automate routine tasks. If a task is repetitive and boring it is almost certainly possible to program a computer to do it, or at least most of it.

■ Integrate processes with other departments. Look at the department handling the stages of the work prior to your department's involvement. It may be more efficient for your department to take over the last part of their processing, or for the other department to take on the first part of yours. The same could apply to the next department's operations.

■ Look for ways to smooth out operations so that staff members aren't idle at some times and impossibly busy at others. For instance, can you do some of the work in advance of when it would normally be done?

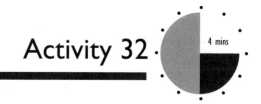

Activity 32

4 mins

As the manager of the checkout team in a medium-sized branch of a supermarket, identify the processes that occur when customers pass through the checkout and recommend at least one way of improving the existing processes.

_____

_____

_____

_____

_____

_____

These are the main processes that I would identify.

■ **Calculate the amount owed by the customer**
Mostly this means picking up an item, finding the barcode, passing it over the scanner and then giving it back to the customer. The computer does the actual calculation. However, there will be a variety of sub-processes to deal with things that don't have a barcode, things whose barcodes can't be read, items that are reduced because they are close to their sell-by date, items that have some damage that is only discovered at the checkout and so on.

■ **Take payment from the customer**
There will be separate sub-processes to deal with payment by cash, cheque, or credit/debit card, processing customer loyalty cards, handling money-off coupons and so on.

■ **Give cash back to the customer, if required**
This process requires the additional input of a signature or initials from the customer and the checkout operator if a credit or debit card is involved.

■ **Liaison with colleagues and managers**
There will be processes for alerting the manager when queues are getting too long, helping out other checkout operators if they run out of change, getting replacements from the shelves for damaged items etc.

■ **Update accounting systems and warehousing systems**
This process is done at the checkout, but in most supermarkets it is entirely automated.

I would say this scenario is one that offers excellent opportunities for bench-marking: just go and shop in another supermarket, and note anything that they do particularly well. Other possible ideas include changing the location or layout of the checkouts, or changing the queuing system so that there is only one queue and the next person in the queue goes to the next available checkout.

4.4 Improving outputs

Your outputs are the products you produce or the services you provide for your internal and/or external customers.

Lots of general things can be done to improve outputs.

■ Keep checking that you know who your customers are and what they want. Maybe your work is received later in the process by a department that has no direct contact with yours, and perhaps does not even know that you are responsible for it. Find out what happens to your work after it leaves you, and if there are extra things you could do, or things you could do differently.

■ Be more flexible: be willing to tailor your product or service to meet special customer demands.

■ See if you can remove any unnecessary parts of the product (for instance decorative features) or pieces of information that are rarely used, so that the product is easier and quicker to create.

■ If you produce several different outputs do they, or could they have, any parts or features in common, or use very similar information? If so, you may be able to save time by using the same component for both products. A simple example would be using the same document template for all the reports you produce.

■ Think about how your product is delivered. If it is information, you can probably deliver it by internal or external email, or perhaps not deliver it physically at all, just make it available on an intranet. If it is a physical product, you may be able to find a faster or more reliable carrier (rail rather than road, for instance). You may find that customers would prefer to come and collect the product. You may even be able to move your department so that it is nearer your customers.

Activity 33 · 4 mins

Yet again you are the manager in charge of the checkout team at a medium-sized branch of a supermarket.

Identify the outputs of the checkout process and recommend at least one way of improving the outputs.

_____

_____

_____

_____

_____

_____

These are my suggestions for outputs.

- The service itself, in other words a customer who has been served in a certain length of time.
- A till receipt and perhaps some money-off coupons.
- Cash back.
- Answers to customer queries such as 'are you open over the Bank Holiday?'
- Occasional help with packing and carrying shopping bags.
- Assistance to colleagues and managers.
- Information for other systems, such as the accounting system, the stock control system and the marketing system.

Most customers will want faster service above all, and there are lots of ways of achieving this, such as 'six items or less' queues and bag packers (assuming they do this more quickly, and as well as, the customer would).

I would like my supermarket to have someone in the checkout area to go and fetch items that I have forgotten to pick up, so I don't lose my place in the queue!

As usual, you probably have your own ideas, depending on your particular gripe with your supermarket.

4.5 Improving staff performance

In 'staff' we include you, of course, because a large part of getting better performance out of people is improving your own management skills. Good management on your part should give you highly motivated and skilled employees. They will work hard for your organization because they realize that if they contribute to your aims, they can achieve their own goals.

> You may like to refer to two other Super Series titles: *Developing Yourself and Others* and *Coaching and Training Your Work Team.*

■ Train your staff. Your organization and its environment are continually changing, so employees constantly need to develop new skills. Training may be needed in a variety of areas: in knowledge about the organization (its mission, objectives, systems, other departments); in personal skills such as time management, decision making, and communication; in specialized knowledge about specific processes in your department or specific tools or software packages that you use; and in general knowledge about matters such as health and safety.

■ Empower your staff. Empowerment means delegating to the lowest possible level, because those most closely involved with operations (the ones who actually do the tasks) are in the best position to make decisions about them. Empowerment leads to faster decisions, helps personal development, and offers staff more job satisfaction.

■ Acknowledge each person's contribution publicly: you'd be surprised how much difference a simple 'thank you' can make. If you are in a position to do so, see that extra effort is rewarded in some way.

■ Encourage teamwork and co-operation. More experienced staff will help with training their less experienced colleagues if both depend on each other to get a job done.

■ Be more open in your communications. Some managers think knowledge is power, but if you keep secrets from people you have no right to be surprised if they don't achieve what you really wanted them to achieve.

■ Think about how you make decisions and whether you can improve. Decisions should be given the attention they deserve, but it is easy to get bogged down in detail.

> For more guidance on managing conflict see *Managing the Employment Relationship.*

■ You can't always make people 'happy', and 'happy' workers aren't necessarily more productive workers. But you can try to make sure that your staff members are treated courteously, without favouritism, prejudice, or public criticism. If you slip, as you probably will, be sure to apologize. If you become aware of a conflict between individual members of staff, bring them together and do everything you can to resolve the conflict. There is nothing worse than an 'atmosphere'.

Activity 34

3 mins

How can you find out whether people need training to improve performance? (You don't have to answer this in relation to the supermarket checkout, but do so if you wish.)

_____

_____

_____

_____

_____

Sometimes it will be obvious. If a new law is passed that affects what an organization does, or new equipment or software is brought in, staff will need to know about it.

Sometimes you may only have hints: absenteeism, high staff turnover, disciplinary issues and frequent mistakes are matters that need to be investigated to see what the root causes are. Training may solve the problem.

Some organizations do formal 'training needs analysis', where training needs are defined as the gap between the requirements of the job and the actual current performance of the people who do it.

Activity 35

30 mins

S/NVQs D6

This activity may provide the basis of appropriate evidence for your S/NVQ portfolio. If you are intending to take this course of action it might be better to write your answers on separate sheets of paper.

Most of the organization management initiatives that have become popular in the last decade or so have, at heart, the idea of the organization as a system made up of lots of smaller inter-related systems and processes.

Describe your part of your organization in this way, in other words identify your work team's inputs, processes and outputs.

Can you identify any way in which these inputs, processes and outputs could be changed so that work activities can be improved? Try to identify ways in which resources can be better controlled by making these changes.

4.6 Quality management initiatives

The need to improve performance is fundamental to most modern organizations, and it won't only be your work team that is expected to improve. The initiative will probably come from very senior managers and will run right through the organization.

Let's look quickly at three organization-wide approaches that you may be expected to contribute to.

EXTENSION 2
If you want to remove some of the theory, and get some good anecdotes, try *101 Ways to Improve Business Performance* by D. Waters. It's also available as an e-book.

■ **Total Quality Management (TQM)**
TQM is a philosophy that the only acceptable quality is perfect quality. This applies to every single resource, process and relationship in the entire organization.

The cost of preventing mistakes is less than the cost of correcting them once they occur. The aim should therefore be to 'get it right first time'.

And even if you do get it right, there is always scope for improvement. The idea of continuous improvement (getting it more right, next time) is a key part of TQM.

■ **ISO 9000**
The ISO 9000 family of standards are set by the International Organization for Standardization, and describe how an organization can set up 'quality management systems' to ensure that quality and customer focus is at the heart of everything the organization does.

If there is a TQM or ISO 9000 initiative in your organization you may find it helpful to look at another workbook in this series, *Providing Quality to Customers*, which covers both in detail.

Organizations that meet ISO 9000's very detailed requirements can arrange to be audited by ISO 9000 Registrars, and get a third-party certificate if they pass.

ISO 9000 is especially important because some types of customer refuse to do business with an organization unless there is some independent assurance of quality. For instance, many government departments and local authorities will only offer contracts to companies that are ISO 9000 certified.

■ The Business Excellence Model

The Business Excellence Model is promoted in the UK by the British Quality Foundation. The model is now more properly known as The EFQM Excellence Model, EFQM being the European Foundation for Quality Management. Organizations can enter an annual competition and win awards for business excellence.

The EFQM Excellence Model, a non-prescriptive framework based on nine criteria, can be used to assess an organization's progress towards excellence. The Model recognizes there are many approaches to achieving sustainable excellence in all aspects of performance. It is based on the premise that:

> **excellent results with respect to Performance, Customers, People and Society are achieved through Leadership driving Policy and Strategy, People, Partnerships and Resources and Processes.**

The model is summarized in the diagram below.

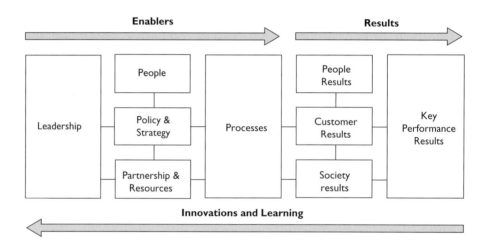

The arrows emphasize the dynamic nature of the model. They show that innovation and learning help to improve enablers which in turn lead to improved results.

For convenience, we use the terms 'Enablers' and 'Results' to designate two categories of criteria. Enabler criteria are concerned with how the organization undertakes key activities; Results criteria are concerned with what results are being achieved.

Applying the model

We can only give a very simplified idea of the model here. More information, including useful free documents to download, is available from the EFQM website on www.efqm.org. The sort of questions you might ask, just to see how well your organization is performing in relation to the criteria shown in the diagram, include the following.

1   How do the behaviour and actions of the executive team and all other leaders inspire, support and promote a culture of Total Quality Management?

2   How does the organization formulate strategies and turn them into plans and actions?

3   How does the organization release the full potential of its people?

4   How does the organization manage resources (especially financial resources) effectively and efficiently?

5   How does the organization deliver value for customers through the management of its processes?

6   What results is the organization achieving in relation to the satisfaction of its external customers?

7   What results is the organization achieving in relation to the satisfaction of its own people?

8   What results is the organization achieving in satisfying the needs and expectations of the community in which it is located?

9   What results is the organization achieving in relation to its planned organization objectives and in satisfying the needs and expectations of everyone with a financial interest in the organization?

Activity 36

To which of the questions in the Business Excellence Model might you give the answer 'via a budgeting system'.

I would say questions 2, 4 and 9 in particular might be answered in this way.

Self-assessment 2

20 mins

1 Who are your internal customers?

_____

_____

_____

2 What is an ideal standard, and what is the drawback of an ideal standard?

_____

_____

_____

3 Fill in the missing words in the following sentences.

   a Monitoring performance is a way of keeping _____ over the activities you are responsible for.

   b When there is a variance from expected performance you should use measures to see where _____ occurred.

4 What should you do if you cannot meet a performance standard due to circumstances beyond your control?

_____

_____

_____

5 Why should improvement be continuous?

_____

_____

_____

_____

6 Suggest three ways of improving processes.

_____

_____

_____

Answers to these questions can be found on pages 117–18.

5 Summary

- To set a performance standard you first need to define performance in overall terms, then find out what is regarded as acceptable performance, and finally define a particular level of performance as the standard.

- The standard set may be an attainable standard – the best you can do at the moment – or you can set more ambitious targets.

- To interpret variances from expected performance standards you first need to identify all the processes and inputs involved in performing tasks, and the relationships between them. You then need to find out what is normal and use measures to see where failures and errors occur.

- Performance reports should concentrate on the exceptions to standard performance.

- Modern organizations need to improve continuously because of fierce competition, ever-changing technology and ever-increasing customer expectations.

- You can see an organization as a system of inputs, processes and outputs. This approach emphasizes that whatever you do has an impact on other parts of the organization.

- You may find yourself taking part in an organization-wide initiative to improve performance such as Total Quality Management, ISO 9000 certification or the EFQM Excellence Model.

Session C
Making work more rewarding

1 Introduction

The main purpose of any system of monitoring has to be improving performance, and the people who can do most to improve performance are the members of your team. In this session we will look at techniques for organizing work that motivate people to work more effectively.

You may have to persuade your line manager to consider some of the changes to work practices before you can introduce them. First, though, we look at a well-established system which adopts quite a different approach.

2 Taking the skill out of work

Organizations have always been interested in efficiency and increased productivity. However, they have not always taken the approach of achieving it by trying to increase staff motivation.

One system that has been widely used is based on what is called the **micro-division of labour**. This system was – and in some cases, still is – employed in factories running automated assembly lines.

The principle behind the micro-division of labour is that jobs are broken down into the smallest possible elements. A high level of automation is used, so the workers perform very simple tasks. This means that almost anyone can very quickly learn to do any particular job with the minimum of training.

Activity 37 · 3 mins

From the point of view of factory efficiency, can you think of some other advantages of this system? Suggest **two** advantages if you can.

_____

_____

_____

_____

Some other advantages are that:

- production does not depend on skilled people and so the absence of any individual does not interfere with the work; in fact, absenteeism is much less of a problem than it is with other systems, because new people can be quickly trained to 'fill in';
- the work is not demanding and so long shifts can be worked – at least, that is the theory;
- the work can be very closely controlled; for instance, if it is found that a certain operation is being done incorrectly it can be quickly traced to a single operator.

So much for the advantages. There is certainly no doubt that factories using this system have been very effective at producing large quantities of goods cheaply.

But there is another side to the story.

There are a number of disadvantages of this system. If we look at it from the production worker's point of view:

- jobs are monotonous and boring;
- unlike machines, people are not very good at doing repetitive work: they lose concentration because they have nothing to keep their interest;

- there's no scope to do the work better or more quickly: machines control the rate of work;
- people who work on assembly lines have little opportunity for social contact.

Activity 38

3 mins

What might be the negative effects of these disadvantages on efficiency? Write down **two** possible effects.

_____

_____

_____

_____

_____

_____

Some of the effects are that:

- when jobs are boring, people tend to make mistakes;
- people who lose concentration are more liable to have accidents;
- where the work is demeaning and there is no scope for personal development, workers may actually become antagonistic towards their employer; this can lead to wildcat strikes and even sabotage (literally putting spanners in the works!);
- there is likely to be a high rate of employee turnover.

All these things will either reduce output or increase costs – or both.

For these reasons and others, many organizations have turned against this system. Instead they have looked for ways of motivating people to take an interest in and responsibility for their work.

3 Reviewing the theory

You may like to refer to the Super Series title *Motivating to Perform in the Workplace*.

At this point we need to review the main theories of motivation:

■ **Maslow's hierarchy of needs**

Maslow showed that people are only preoccupied with basic survival and safety when these things are under threat. Otherwise, they tend to 'climb' to greater goals and needs, including a sense of belonging, self-respect and self-fulfilment.

■ **Theory X and Theory Y**

McGregor proposed that, rather than disliking work and responsibility, people will, under the right conditions, enjoy work and seek responsibility. They prefer to control and direct themselves, rather than being regulated from above.

■ **Herzberg's two-factor theory**

A fairly recent concept in management is that of **empowerment**, which, in broad terms, means managers stepping back and giving individuals and work teams the power to organize their own work. Empowerment could be said to be a realization of McGregor's ideas under Theory Y.

Herzberg's work indicates that the factors causing job satisfaction are not the same as those causing dissatisfaction. The motivators – such as recognition, responsibility and job interest – can be found in an employee's relationship to what he or she does. The maintenance factors – such as working conditions, salary and status – are more to do with the work environment.

■ **Expectancy theory**

This refers to the expectations of an employee and the cycle of cause and effect between motivation, effort, performance and reward. If the reward does not provide the motivation, the motivation does not lead to effort, the effort does not result in the required performance, then the reward will not be earned.

■ **Hackman and Oldham**

This theory is best summed up in this table:

The essential job characteristics:	What the worker gets from them:	The result, if all these job characteristics are present:
Feedback from job	→ Knowledge of the actual results of the work activities	
Autonomy	→ Experienced responsibility for outcomes of the work	High internal work motivation
Skill variety Task identity Task significance	→ Experienced meaningfulness of the work	

When this theory is applied to the practice of de-skilling, it suggests people will perform badly and react against the system and the organization.

The main problem with the micro-division of labour is that the jobs are designed as if people were robots, and not very clever robots at that. Many organizations have now moved completely away from this idea, and have redesigned their workplaces to be more efficient by **enriching** jobs, rather than simplifying them.

4 Job enrichment

There is now a trend towards **job enrichment** (although this particular term may not be used by all organizations). Job enrichment means designing work and workplaces so that people have:

■ more responsibility;
■ more scope for self-development;
■ more control over the work they do;
■ more feedback on results.

Activity 39

3 mins

Which of the theories above tend to support the trend towards job enrichment?

_____

_____

I would say that those of McGregor, Maslow, Herzberg, and Hackman and Oldham all do.

- McGregor's Theory Y put up the idea that people like work and responsibility.
- Maslow suggested that people have greater needs than simply survival and security.
- Herzberg showed that job interest, achievement, recognition, responsibility and advancement were the main motivators.
- Hackman and Oldham suggested that feedback, responsibility and meaningfulness are all requirements for motivation.

But before we continue any further on this theme, let us clarify what job enrichment **is** and what it **is not**.

5 Job rotation and job enlargement

'The utility man typically has no more self-control, only slightly more knowledge of results and only a slightly greater chance to test his valued abilities.' – Edward E. Lawler, (1969) _Job Design and Employee Motivation._

Job enrichment should not be confused with two other approaches to job redesign: job **rotation** and job **enlargement.**

Job rotation involves switching people between a number of different jobs of relatively similar complexity. An example of this would be to allow production workers to swap from one part of the assembly line to another.

Although job rotation has the advantage of increasing flexibility, **it does not increase motivation**. A young bank employee summed it up when she said:

'After I'd been at the bank a few months I became bored with my job. They introduced job rotation and now I move from one boring job to another!'

Job enlargement involves adding more tasks of similar complexity to the job. Once again, **motivation is not improved**. Applied to our bank clerk, she might well have said:

'**After I'd been at the bank a few months I became bored with my job. They introduced job enlargement and now I have several more boring tasks added to the job!'**

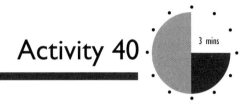

Activity 40

3 mins

Bearing in mind the theory we've covered, what reason can you give for job rotation and job enlargement failing to motivate?

_____

_____

_____

_____

EXTENSION 3
Charles B. Handy discusses job design and job enlargement in his book *Understanding Organizations*.

I hope you agree that job rotation and job enlargement both fail to motivate because they do not offer the opportunity for growth. Doing more things or different things of the same complexity does not allow people to build on experience and knowledge.

Job enrichment, on the other hand, does just that. We can first look at it in terms of the Hackman and Oldham theory. It generally involves:

- adding **skill variety**, by increasing the number of complex tasks to a job over a period of time. Such tasks are designed to give people the chance to develop underused skills and abilities;
- providing increased **task significance**: designing the work to be important, so that others depend on its outcome. (Organizations encourage staff to see others as customers of their work, these days, which fits in well with the idea of increased task significance);
- presenting new tasks as **opportunities** rather than demands. This offers a degree of choice as to what tasks to do and when to do them. More complex tasks can be taken on as and when people feel able to cope;
- giving people and teams greater **autonomy**: allowing more discretion in the way that the job is paced, checked, sequenced and so on. You may hear the word **empowerment**, which, as mentioned earlier, means managers stepping back and giving work teams the power to run themselves;
- setting up systems that ensure fast, direct **feedback**.

When designing for job enrichment, Maslow's work must also be borne in mind: people won't be ready to satisfy these 'higher' needs if more basic wants have not been satisfied.

And our reading of Herzberg should remind us that maintenance or hygiene factors may get in the way of motivation.

What about expectancy theory? That tells us that staff should be able to see that:

- there is a link between effort and performance, and between performance and reward;
- the distribution of rewards is fair;
- rewards are worth having, in their own eyes.

6 Job enrichment in practice

Let us look at two very different examples of job enrichment in practice.

6.1 The case of W.H. Smith & Sons (Tools) Ltd

W.H. Smith & Sons (Tools) Ltd is medium-sized, family owned business (completely unrelated to the well-known high street retailer). It started out in 1933 as a machine tool maker in the original W.H. Smith's shed, but during the 1990s the company expanded dramatically, with turnover increased from £9m to £24m. It achieved this by using its main strength – it has the largest in-house tool room in the UK – to offer a complete service from tool-making through plastic injection moulding to final assembly. It supplies components and sub-assemblies to leading brands like Black and Decker, Motorola and Triton.

But this growth didn't happen without a struggle. In 1991 Nissan, a new customer, awarded them a score of just one out of ten in an audit. Colin Sarson, the Managing Director was shocked. This assessment of their performance was replicated by Black and Decker and by Rover, and led the company to look carefully at what it did and how it did it. As Colin says, he had to relearn his own style of managing, to recognize that he needed to communicate better and listen to what people in the factory had to say.

Colin also had to demonstrate that the concerns of employees were treated seriously. When people complained about puddles in the car park, or dirty toilets, something had to be done about them, to win over people to the idea that their views mattered. This change in the culture of the organization, realigning all employees – managers and factory floor alike – to be committed to improvement, demands a demonstration of commitment from the top.

The company changed to a 'cell' structure, with each cell having full responsibility for supplying a particular customer. The advantage of this approach is that the focus of the whole cell is on the customer, rather than looking inwards at other production functions. An example of this is W.H. Smith's Triton cell. Parts for Triton are supplied direct from the W.H. Smith line to the Triton line. This is based on the *kanban* approach developed by Toyota and is a form of *just-in-time* operations. The link between the customer's production line and the supplier's line is direct and is managed on an hourly basis by the personnel directly involved in the process. By shortening communication lines, stockholding is minimized and the customer has the flexibility needed to respond directly to consumer demand.

To support this, W.H. Smith invested heavily in training and development. Responsibility for staffing is devolved direct to the cell management (the company doesn't have a personnel department) and all employees go through an initial induction programme that feeds into a personel development plan, agreed individually with line managers. This is accompanied by a right to one hour per week's (paid) time to learn. For the company, investment in its people is seen as being at least as important as its investment in machinery and buildings.

The employees now have a high level of responsibility for their own work and the quality of the products they produce. They are constantly seeking new ways to improve quality and reduce costs, and the company has achieved significant improvements in output and reduced staff turnover.

6.2 Enriched jobs in voluntary work

Rani Akinyemi and Betty Dunphy are volunteers working in a centre caring for children with learning disabilities. During the course of a typical week, they get:

Skill variety. They're expected to carry out a variety of tasks around the centre, which exercise their skills in a number of ways, including:

- manual work;
- planning skills (e.g. for outings);
- communicating skills;
- calculating skills (Betty often helps out with the accounts);
- caring skills;
- cooking skills.

Task identity. For the most part, they are expected to complete whole tasks.

Task significance. They are aware that the children and others depend on them, sometimes critically.

Autonomy. There aren't enough people for there to be much close supervision, so Rani and Betty are relied upon to organize their work as they see fit.

Feedback from the job. The most rewarding feedback is to see the children respond to them, and show real affection.

Needless to say, Rani and Betty are highly motivated!

Before you go on to the next session, which is about the team leader's role, try the Self-assessment questions opposite.

Self-assessment 3

10 mins

Fill in the blanks in the sentences on the left with the correct phrases taken from the list in capitals below.

AUTONOMY, COMPLEXITY, FEEDBACK FROM THE JOB,
JOB ROTATION, JOB ENLARGEMENT, MICRO-DIVISION OF LABOUR,
SKILL VARIETY, SMALLEST, TASKS, TASK IDENTITY, TASK SIGNIFICANCE

1 The principle behind the _____ is that jobs are broken down into the _____ possible elements.

2 Job enrichment means designing jobs so that people have more _____, _____, _____, _____, and _____.

3 _____ involves switching people between a number of different jobs of relatively similar _____.

4 _____ involves adding more _____ of similar complexity to the job.

For questions 5 to 8, decide whether each statement is TRUE, FALSE or SOMETIMES TRUE.

5 When jobs are broken down into very simple tasks that anyone can learn, the problem of staff turnover becomes unimportant: you 'just recruit more people off the street'. TRUE/FALSE/SOMETIMES TRUE

6 Job enrichment is very hard to implement, because it entails lots of training to do more complex tasks. TRUE/FALSE/SOMETIMES TRUE

7 Job enrichment programmes should be presented as opportunities, not demands. TRUE/FALSE/SOMETIMES TRUE

8 Small organizations can't implement job enrichment programmes, as they have not the resources of large companies. TRUE/FALSE/SOMETIMES TRUE

9 Which of the following ideas support the concept of job enrichment?

   a Herzberg's theory that job interest is a motivator.
   b Maslow's theory that people who are starving have no interest in self-development.
   c McGregor's Theory X: that people dislike work and responsibility.
   d McGregor's Theory Y: that people prefer to control themselves than be controlled from above.
   e Hackman and Oldham's theories about the prerequisites for internal motivation.

The answers to these questions can be found on page 118.

7 Summary

- The **micro-division of labour** is the breaking down of jobs into their simplest possible elements. It is ultimately inefficient.

- **Job rotation** is the switching of people between jobs of similar complexity.

- **Job enlargement** involves adding more tasks of similar complexity to a job.

- **Job enrichment** means designing jobs so that people have:

  - skill variety;
  - task identity;
  - task significance;
  - autonomy;
  - feedback from the job.

Session D
The team leader's role

1 Introduction

Team leaders have a vital role in motivating people. It might almost be said that this is their main function, for a team that is not motivated will invariably perform badly. The team leader is, among other things:

- a coach, who aims to bring out the best in people;
- a facilitator, who clears away obstacles to enable the team to make unimpeded progress;
- an empowering agent, providing the team with the skills and information to manage themselves.

Whatever your title, you are a team leader if you run a team.

In this part of the workbook we are going to discuss how the ideas of motivation we've covered can be applied by team leaders.

2 Needs and your team

Abraham Maslow identified five levels of human needs or goals:

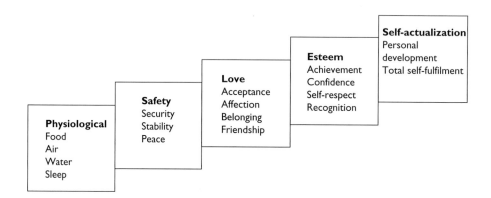

Let's look at the ways in which rewards of work can help to satisfy each of these needs.

Activity 41

8 mins

List up to **two** things which can be provided by an organization (such as yours) for its employees or volunteers, in order to help satisfy **each** level of Maslow's needs. I have included an example of each in the list below.

Physiological

■ canteen facilities

■ _____

■ _____

Safety

■ safe working conditions

■ _____

■ _____

Love

■ the chance to work in a group

■ _____

■ _____

Esteem

■ praise for work done

■ _____

■ _____

Self-actualization

■ interesting work

■ _____

■ _____

Answers to these questions can be found on pages 119–20.

Team leaders can't always control the provision of all these things, although they may be able to have a strong influence.

Let's now go on to look at some of the ways in which team leaders can play a direct part in motivating members of their teams.

3 Motivation and the team

Whether you are an appointed team leader, or were elected as leader of a self-managed team, you have to try to ensure that each person in your work team is able to perform at work in the best way possible. This probably involves a series of complex tasks, which may include:

■ planning work in advance;
■ organizing things so that materials and equipment are available when and where they're needed;
■ making sure team members are properly trained;
■ providing clear information about what is required;
■ giving feedback on results.

As we have been discussing, perhaps more than anything else it involves helping them to find the motivation to do the job well.

We have talked about job enrichment, but it is important to remember that different things motivate different people: there is no straightforward answer to the question:

'How do I motivate my team members?'

Activity 42 · 3 mins

How can you find out what motivates each member of your work team? Make **one** suggestion.

_____

_____

_____

_____

You might have suggested simply asking them. This is one approach. But will they be able to tell you? Our dictionary definition of motivation was 'A conscious or unconscious driving force. . . .': people aren't always aware of what motivates them.

A more realistic suggestion is to

get to know the members of your team

in order to get an understanding of what they want and expect from work. Of course, this statement is very easily made, but may not be so easy to put into practice.

Activity 43

3 mins

Can you write down **one** reason why a team leader may find it hard to get to know team members well?

_____

_____

_____

For one thing, there is often a perceived status gap between a team leader and the rest of the team, which may get in the way of a true and complete understanding of attitudes and values.

Another thing that gets in the way of knowing people is that many people hide their real feelings.

A further difficulty is that the needs and attitudes of people aren't necessarily fixed. It is dangerous to assume that someone will react the same way to a set of circumstances in the future to the way she or he has reacted in the past.

Nevertheless, if you want to be able to provide the motivation the team members want, there's no effective alternative to talking with them, working with them and observing them in action.

3.1 What the team leader can do

Returning to the question of what you can do, as a team leader, to motivate your team members, let's summarize the areas where you might have the opportunity to take some actions.

■ **Engender the right kind of climate or atmosphere.**

The atmosphere of an organization is determined by the policies of management and by the attitudes of everyone working there. Local team leaders do have some control over atmosphere within the group or section where they operate. If you are willing to adopt an open, sharing approach to your team and your work, there's a good chance others will do the same. Don't expect overnight miracles, however!

■ **Give rewards where they're deserved.**

Activity 44

4 mins

Think for a few minutes of what rewards you can offer your team. Remember that motivation is derived from the expectation of a reward, but that rewards do not have to be tangible ones.

Try to suggest **three** rewards that you might offer.

_____

_____

_____

Any team leader can reward the members of his or her team by:

- being generous in **praise** of their achievements;
- giving **thanks** for efforts made and personal contributions made;
- giving feedback in the form of **constructive criticism** – a point we'll expand upon shortly;
- recognizing the needs of the **individual**, and the part played by each person in the collective effort, rather than treating people as if they were all the same;
- trying to improve **social** relationships, by, for example, setting out work areas so that it is easy for team members to communicate;
- giving **recognition** of extra effort;
- giving **responsibility** where it is deserved and wanted.

It may be in your power to bestow many other rewards. They may range from buying a team member a drink to putting up someone's name for promotion.

- **Promote the intrinsic worth of the job.**

We have seen that 'task significance' is an essential ingredient for high motivation. One of your functions, as team leader, is to 'sell' to the team the inherent value of the job they are doing, and point out the ways in which the outcome affects others.

■ **Keep the work team informed.**

Your team members will want to feel fully involved in the organization they work for, and will take a professional interest in events and reports concerning the kind of work they do. You can play a part in keeping them abreast of developments.

■ **Be fair in allocating work.**

One thing that can get in the way of motivation is a perceived unfairness in task allocation: 'She gets all the easy jobs. I have to struggle through with the horrible ones'.

There's nothing surprising in this kind of reaction. We have already discussed the fact that status is a maintenance factor; perceived inequities in work assignment are often interpreted as a difference in the position of one person compared with another.

■ **Make work fun.**

You may not agree with this suggestion. Work is important to most people, and may be taken very seriously. But it doesn't mean you can't be light-hearted, enjoy a joke, and see the humorous side of things. If you can manage to make work fun, you will have gone a long way to motivating your team.

■ **Take account of the circumstances under which people have to work.**

Few of us are lucky enough to work in an ideal environment, where all the resources we need are available to us. You, as a leader, may be unable to provide the working conditions you would like to. Your team may include one or more of the following groups, for example: volunteers; short-term contract staff; part-time staff; temporary employees.

The motivation of an unpaid volunteer will be rather different from a permanent member of staff building a long-term career. The volunteer may be self-motivated to a large extent, but will nevertheless still need plenty of support and encouragement.

Temporary and part-time staff may not feel that they are part of the team at all, and are very often treated as though they have no need of motivation beyond their pay. If you can spend a little time in giving such staff background information, and show that you value their contribution, you may be surprised at how much better motivated they can be.

■ **Give your team members scope for development.**

For many workers, the main attraction of a job is the opportunities it offers for development and growth. This is particularly true of young people, and when the job is poorly paid (or not paid at all). You can:

■ look out for suitable openings for team members, within the job or in other parts of the organization;
■ give information and training which will enable people to develop their talents;
■ encourage and help individuals to take available, and appropriate opportunities.

■ **Avoid threats to security.**

As Herzberg observed, job insecurity is a threat and a demotivating factor. We discussed already the fact that most people are not normally motivated by the fact of having a job, but may become very demotivated should there be a threat of losing it.

■ **Make the team's targets and objectives clear.**

Even teams with a high degree of autonomy need to be reminded what they are trying to achieve. Having a clear goal is a great motivator.

3.2 Motivation in an uncertain atmosphere

You may have been in the position of seeing:

■ the organization being 'rationalized' or down-sized;
■ colleagues being made redundant;
■ uncertainty about the economic future of the organization.

How do you keep up morale and motivation in these circumstances?

Some suggestions to add to your own ideas are:

■ seeking information, and passing on as clear a picture of the situation as you are able, because anxiety feeds on doubt, and rumours tend to abound when there's no clear message coming through;
■ countering cynicism with a positive approach that encourages people to make the best of things as they are, and to plan for the future;
■ keeping the team occupied with meaningful work – which, where others have been made redundant, there is probably no shortage of – but not letting them get overwhelmed;

- in the case of those who have been left behind when friends and colleagues have been 'let go', acknowledging and discussing the guilt that is likely to be felt;
- talking with people and establishing new, mutually supportive relationships;
- treating one another with respect.

4 Managing performance to meet objectives

You have seen earlier in this workbook that one of the things you can do, as a team leader, to motivate people – and so improve performance – is to set clear objectives. But it's no good just handing over a set of objectives and leaving people to get on with it – this might in fact have the opposite of the desired effect and actually demotivate them. Instead you need to follow a process in which team members are actively engaged and supported in each of the following steps:

- establish clear objectives for the team;
- establish clear objectives for each individual;
- identify what obstacles individuals need to overcome in order to meet their objectives and how you can help them in this;
- maintain ongoing communication and exchange of information;
- give regular feedback.

The first two steps focus on writing clear objectives. So before we look at each step in more detail we will consider exactly what a 'clear objective' is.

4.1 Writing clear objectives

Writing clear objectives, whether for a department/team or individual, is an art in itself. A frequently-used way of ensuring they are clear is to apply what is known as the SMART principle, which means that they are:

- Specific
- Measurable
- Achievable
- Relevant
- Time bound.

A *specific* objective is one that states precisely what is to be achieved. For example, 'We will increase the speed with which we respond to customers' phone calls' is much too vague. To make this specific you need to state how quickly you will aim to respond – for example. 'We will respond to customers' phone calls within six rings'.

A *measurable* objective is one whose achievement is easy to assess. For example, you can assess the achievement of the objective that 'No customer will have to wait more than 5 minutes to be seen after arriving at the reception desk' by keeping a record of exactly how long each customer has to wait. But if the objective is that 'No customer will have to wait an unreasonable length of time to be seen' you have a problem. Without a definition of 'unreasonable' how can you determine whether the objective is met?

An *achievable* objective is one that can be attained given the current situation and the available skills and resources. Over-ambitious objectives can be demotivating, raising expectations that cannot be met. However, this does not mean that they should be set so low that little effort will be required to attain them.

An objective should be *relevant* in two ways: it should relate to the individual's job and be of significance to the organization.

Every objective must be *time bound* – that is, state precisely when something is to be achieved. At the end of the time limit, progress towards achievement will need to be reviewed. If the objective has been achieved, a new one should be set. If it has not been achieved, the reasons need to be examined. If it appears that it was unrealistic, a new and more achievable objective should be set.

Activity 45

3 mins

Casey is an operations analyst in a bank. She has been given a number of objectives, all of which are achievable and relevant. But which ones are also specific, measurable and time bound? Put ticks in the relevant boxes.

Objective	Specific	Measurable	Time bound
Respond to all enquiries from clients within 24 hours			
Develop an understanding of the German domestic market			
Collect information by 30 June on what procedures should be in place for processing transactions with Germany			
Ensure by 30 June that all internal enquiries receive a response within 24 hours			

The first objective is certainly specific and measurable, but despite the reference to 'within 24 hours' it is not time bound as it does not say by what date the objective is to be achieved. The second objective is obviously not time bound. It is also not specific as it does not define exactly what it is about the German market that is to be understood. Furthermore, it is not measurable: it does not state how achievement of understanding is to be assessed. The third objective is time bound. However, it does not state what type of transactions the information is to be collected about, or how much information is to be collected, so it is neither specific nor measurable. Only the fourth objective meets all three criteria.

4.2 Meeting to agree team objectives

In some work situations you may find that objectives are handed down to you by senior managers. However, ideally you and your team should be able to work together in formulating your objectives for the coming year. In doing so it is essential to be aware of the organization's overall goals and objectives. To return to the example of Casey in Activity 45, one of the goals of the bank she works for is to provide unparalleled levels of service to its clients, and for the coming year, one of its objectives is to increase its customer base by 10 per cent. Consequently, Casey and her colleagues need to focus on the part they can play in increasing client satisfaction. The manager has found that in the last few months some clients have had to wait for up to two days for a response to an enquiry. In discussion with the team it is agreed that they will increase client satisfaction considerably if they aim to respond to all enquiries within 24 hours.

4.3 Meeting to agree individual objectives, obstacles and responsibilities

In any meeting with an individual team member to agree their objectives, you may find it useful to have to hand not only the departmental/team objectives, but also the individual's job description and the outcomes of their last performance appraisal. There is no point in agreeing objectives that are either outside the scope of the individual's job or that they are simply not capable of achieving.

This does not mean, of course, that the tasks individuals are required to undertake should never change. To return to the example of Casey once again, it is apparent that if the objective of responding to customer's enquiries within 24 hours is to be achieved, various procedures will have to be made more efficient. Computer-based as most of Casey's work is, she still uses time-consuming manual methods to carry out particular tasks. She needs a more thorough knowledge of working with Excel spreadsheets and setting up macros if she is to reduce the amount of manual work she does. Consequently, she agrees with her manager that she needs further training in this area and her manager undertakes to organize it.

One of the final things to consider is whether there is any need to revise the individual's job description. Returning to Casey, it has become apparent that Casey is regarded by her colleagues as a reliable source of support and advice on how to complete a wide range of tasks. She has said that she has no ambitions to become a first line manager. However, if the department is to meet its objective of dealing with all enquiries within 24 hours, it is vital that she continues to play the role of mentor. The best course of action is to recognize that she does this and write it into her job description (possibly with consequences for her rate of pay).

Activity 46

Select one or more of your own job objectives and analyse each of them by considering the following questions.

a Is the objective specific?   YES/NO

b Is the objective measurable?   YES/NO

c Is the objective achievable and realistic?   YES/NO

d Is the objective relevant?   YES/NO

e Is the objective time bound?   YES/NO

If you answered 'no' to question a, you might like to consider how it could be made more specific.

If you answered 'no' to question b, you might like to consider how it could be made more measurable.

If you answered 'no' to questions c, d or e, you might like to consider why this is the case.

4.4 Maintaining communication

Once an individual's objectives have been agreed, it is essential to maintain a dialogue with them in which information is shared on actual and potential obstacles to progress. This is not only for the benefit of the individual team member but also for you in your role of co-ordinating the work of the people whom you supervise. Once you know what the problems are you will be able to discuss possible solutions with staff and, if necessary, with your manager.

At the same time, you can give them feedback on how they are doing, always taking care to adopt a constructive approach. We will return to the subject of feedback in the next section.

There are both formal and informal methods of maintaining communication. Formal methods include:

- regular written reports
- team meetings
- regular one-to-one meetings.

Activity 47 · 6 mins

What do you think are the advantages and disadvantages of each of these formal methods of communication?

	Advantages	Disadvantages
Regular written reports		
Team meetings		
One-to-one meetings		

Regular written reports can be helpful if you and a staff member often do not work in the same place. However, they can also become time-wasting and one-way, with the member of staff keeping you informed while you provide little in return. If you are pressed for time, team meetings in which each person discusses how they are doing with regard to their objectives can provide opportunities to discuss ways in which other people can help. However, they are no substitute for one-to-one meetings in which problems can be discussed frankly. For both types of meeting, it is essential to keep a brief record of what is discussed and agreed.

The main informal method of communication is known as 'management by walking around', where you talk to staff as you come across them. This can be very beneficial, for it means that problems can be discussed and solved as they occur. However, it can also cause problems if staff are made to feel that they should always wait for you to come to them rather that be able to come to you with a problem. It is important to be clear about the situations in which staff can in fact do this.

4.5 Giving feedback

Direct feedback from the job can be an important motivator. However, many individuals and teams are unable to get sufficient feedback from the job itself. Therefore, they rely on the team leader to provide feedback on **how** they are doing in achieving their objectives – and not simply on **whether** they are doing well. The challenge for you is to give feedback in a way that will get a positive response – no matter whether the feedback is positive or negative.

A formal way of giving feedback is by holding an annual (or possibly six-monthly) appraisal meeting. Appraisal meetings are the subject of a separate book entitled *Motivating to Perform in the Workplace*. Here we will concentrate on giving feedback in less formal situations and on a more frequent basis.

In preparing to give someone feedback, bear in mind the following principles:

■ Negative criticism on its own generally has a bad effect. Always balance the negative with something positive. The best course of action is usually to start with a positive comment before saying something negative, and to end with another positive comment.
■ Give feedback on a particular piece of work immediately after it has been completed.
■ Don't be too vague. Difficult as it is, make sure you are clear about what the problem is.

■ Focus on what the person has *done* rather than how they have appeared to be. For example, if someone has given the appearance of being rather bored by the task of writing up a report – but nevertheless has produced a good-quality piece of work – concentrate on this rather than on their attitude.

■ Focus on what the person has done in specific situations. Do not assume that because they have behaved in a particular way in one situation, they will always behave this way in similar situations.

■ Focus on sharing ideas and exploring alternative courses of action rather than telling the other person what you think they should do.

■ Finally, make sure that any action you promise to undertake yourself is actually carried out.

Activity 48

How often do you let individual team members know how well they are doing?

Most of the time   ❏

On the odd occasion   ❏

How often do you feed back information about the effects the team's work has had, by (say) telling them how well received it was by a customer or another department?

Most of the time   ❏

On the odd occasion   ❏

If you don't tell them often enough, how will they get to know? Everybody needs to know how well they are achieving objectives, and what the results of their work are. They need to be able to see, too, that the outcome of their work is having a significant effect on the lives of others.

Let's look at an example of the constructive role feedback can play in improving performance. A professional singer who performs publicly will get a certain amount of feedback from the audience. If there is rapturous applause at the end of a performance, the singer will be pleased with herself, because she will know that she has sung well. Even then, however, the singer may be conscious of certain flaws in her performance, and worried whether there were any others she has not noticed. She will probably want to find ways to improve her delivery: the next audience may not be so easily pleased!

For these reasons, the singer may look to others for constructive criticism: her music teacher, the producer of the concert or show, colleagues, professional critics and friends. She may also spend hours listening to recordings of her own voice. The singer, like anyone else desiring to improve their performance, is very interested in getting detailed feedback about the results of her work.

It goes without saying that all criticism should be given with tact and diplomacy, and the critic must be careful not to trigger any negative reactions.

One of the characters in the novel *Of Human Bondage*, by W. Somerset Maugham, said: 'People ask you for criticism, but they only want praise'. Is this your experience?

Activity 49

S/NVQ D6

If you develop your responses into a detailed plan, it would form useful evidence for your S/NVQ portfolio. If you are intending to take this course of action, it might be better to write your answers on separate sheets of paper.

Write down answers to the following questions. What changes do you intend to make:

■ to the frequency or timing of feedback you give to your team?

_____

_____

_____

■ in the method you use to give feedback to your team members, i.e., the way that you convey the messages?

_____

_____

_____

■ in the content of the feedback messages you give to your team?

_____

_____

_____

5 Job enrichment

How much influence and control you have when it comes to introducing job enrichment depends on the kind of work you do and the kind of organization you work for.

What is important is that you recognize the value of job enrichment and promote and encourage it whenever and wherever you can.

5.1 Job enrichment in your workplace

The following activity will help you to focus on job enrichment in your workplace.

Activity 50 · 3 mins

The list below suggests some ways in which job enrichment might be introduced. Place a tick against each item which you think you might have the authority or influence to implement for your team.

a Letting the work team members see a job through from start to finish. ☐

b Enhancing task significance. ☐

c Increasing levels of responsibility. ☐

d Reducing the level of supervision, giving the team members greater control over the work. ☐

e Providing more feedback over results. ☐

f Introducing greater skill variety, perhaps by increasing the range of tasks by delegation. ☐

g Giving an individual the opportunity to become expert in some specific task. ☐

5.2 Would it work?

Is job enrichment right for your team? Introducing a programme of job enrichment can be a big step. You will need to think about what you want to achieve and how best to achieve it.

Go through the following checklist to help you decide whether embarking on a job enrichment programme could be right for your team.

Activity 51

2 mins

Answer the following questions.

a Do you believe the jobs of your team   YES   NO
   members can be enriched?

b Will they take up the opportunities offered by   YES   NO
   their enriched job?

c Will a job enrichment programme improve   YES   NO
   performance?

d Will management support you if you embark   YES   NO
   on a job enrichment programme?

e Will training be required?   YES   NO

a In general, the answer must be YES. All evidence suggests that any job can be enriched.

b That's your judgement. Not everyone is looking for job enrichment, but most people welcome it.

c Experience shows that it usually does. Herzberg demonstrated in a number of studies that job enrichment achieves increased productivity.

d Crucial question! An extensive programme should not be undertaken lightly.

e The changes you introduce may not be possible without an associated training programme. If you are restricted on the amount of training you can provide, this fact should be taken into account.

5.3 Which jobs?

What kind of jobs would lend themselves to job enrichment?

Look at jobs where:

- job satisfaction is low;
- maintenance factors are costly;
- changes would not be expensive;
- lack of motivation is affecting performance.

Activity 52

List the jobs done by your team which meet some or all of these criteria.

- Jobs where job satisfaction is low are:

_____

_____

_____

_____

S/NVQ D6

- Jobs where maintenance factors are costly are:

_____

_____

_____

_____

- Jobs where changes would not be expensive are:

_____

_____

_____

_____

■ Jobs where lack of motivation is affecting performance are:

_____

_____

_____

_____

■ Select the jobs that appear on at least two of these lists. They may be the best ones for job enrichment.

_____

_____

_____

_____

5.4 How can you devise appropriate changes?

One technique is to try 'brainstorming' – listing as many changes as you can that may enrich the job **even if they seem impossible to apply**. Brainstorming is usually thought of as a group activity, but it can be almost as useful to work on your own. Take a blank sheet of paper and write down all the possible ways you can think of to enrich the jobs of your team. Then, when you've run out of ideas, eliminate:

■ those changes that involve maintenance factors, rather than motivation factors;
■ those changes which, for some clear reason, are not practical;
■ those changes which appear to be job enlargement, rather than job enrichment.

5.5 How should the changes be presented?

Present them as **opportunities**

5.6 How can you decide whether the changes are effective?

You should find ways of **measuring** the result of the changes. One approach is to set up a 'controlled experiment' in order to measure the success or otherwise of job enrichment programmes. You may feel you do not have time for such a trial. Nevertheless, it is vital that you establish some way of measuring the change in performance.

Activity 53

S/NVQ D6

This Activity will provide you with a basis for a structured approach to the assessment of development activities. If you develop your responses into a detailed plan, it would form useful evidence for your S/NVQ portfolio. If you are intending to take this course of action, it might be better to write your answers on separate sheets of paper.

Some ways of measuring are listed below. Tick those that you think would be appropriate to you.

- by volume of production ☐
- by number of sales made ☐
- by number of customer complaints ☐
- by value of work produced ☐
- by quality of work produced ☐
- by value of sales ☐
- by amount of wastage or scrap ☐
- by bonus earned ☐
- by amount of rework ☐
- by cost per unit produced ☐
- by reduction in absenteeism ☐
- by reduction in lateness ☐
- by reduction in lost time through accidents ☐

My ideas for measuring changes would be

_____

_____

_____

_____

5.7 How soon can you expect to see results?

When introducing job enrichment, be prepared for some initial drop in performance – don't forget that people may take a while to get used to the new ideas. However, this effect should not last for long and you should not let it deter you.

6 Job enrichment and the team

There are things that can be done to introduce job enrichment, which team leaders have the power to implement. They include:

■ delegating tasks and responsibilities, so that team members have more control over their work;
■ increasing autonomy by modifying the level of supervision given.

Let us examine each of these more closely.

6.1 Delegating

Along with other team leaders, you are able to exercise some control over the work of your team.

You also have the choice of doing all your own work yourself or allowing your work team to take on some of it.

In other words, you can **delegate** some of your own work and/or your responsibilities.

You may find the following procedure helpful in the process of delegation.

a Make a list of tasks and responsibilities that you normally do yourself, which might possibly be delegated. Don't forget to include those jobs you never quite get around to doing!

b Make sure you haven't included those jobs which you can't delegate – such as responsibility for safety.

c Consider allocating the tasks to specific team members, by answering the questions:

'Is this task within the capability of this individual? If so, would he or she find it challenging and rewarding?'

d Allocate the task, making clear what is to be achieved. Provide training where necessary.

e Follow up by checking that people aren't in difficulties and that progress is being made.

f Do not use delegation as an excuse to get rid of jobs you dislike doing. Never delegate anything you are not prepared to do yourself.

Like all job enrichment, delegated tasks are an opportunity; they shouldn't be made into demands.

Remember too that:

you can't avoid the responsibility for a task by getting others to do it for you.

If you are interested in finding out more about how to delegate, you might consider studying *Solving Problems and Making Decisions* in this series.

6.2 Giving your team members more scope

Increasing autonomy is a significant step towards job enrichment.

Activity 54

S/NVQ
D6

You could develop this Activity to cover each member of your team. This will give you a plan for giving your team greater autonomy and control, thereby encouraging and stimulating them to make the best use of their abilities. If you develop your responses into a detailed plan, it would form useful evidence for your S/NVQ portfolio. If you are intending to take this course of action, it might be better to write your answers on separate sheets of paper.

To what extent is your work team controlled? Take a few minutes and think about the work done by **one** member of your team. Then tick the appropriate boxes. Next, for each of the NOT AT ALL answers, say what actions you intend to take to give the team member greater control.

Job title _____

To what extent can he or she:	NOT AT ALL	TO SOME DEGREE	A GOOD DEAL

■ control the pace of the work?
Proposed actions _____
_____

■ determine the order or sequence in
  which the work is done?
Proposed actions _____
_____

■ decide how the work is done?
Proposed actions _____
_____

■ decide when the work is done?
Proposed actions _____
_____

■ choose the tools, equipment or
  materials used for the job?
Proposed actions _____
_____

■ influence the quality of work produced?
Proposed actions _____
_____

■ decide where the work is done?
Proposed actions _____
_____

By giving the team the opportunity for greater autonomy, you may feel you will lose control completely! The key is in careful planning: you need to be sure that the changes will work, and you must be ready to support team members when they need you. You cannot afford to sacrifice achievement of the team's objectives, simply in order to increase motivation; if you do, it is likely to have the opposite effect. The question that you have to answer is: 'How do I enrich the jobs of my team, and thereby increase their efficiency and effectiveness?'

Self-assessment 4 · 10 mins

1 What advice would you give to a colleague at the same level as you who wanted to motivate his or her team? Say whether you think each of the following would be good or bad advice, and then explain your reasoning.

   a 'Get to know your team members well.'   GOOD/BAD

   _____

   _____

   b 'Try to improve their working conditions.'   GOOD/BAD

   _____

   _____

   c 'Give them more scope and more involvement.'   GOOD/BAD

   _____

   _____

   d 'Watch them more closely, so they know you care
      about them.'   GOOD/BAD

   _____

   _____

2 Which of the following statements are true and which are false?

   a A SMART objective is short, measurable, achievable,
     relevant and time bound.   TRUE/FALSE

   b The best form of ongoing communication regarding
     work performance is one-to-one meetings.   TRUE/FALSE

   c When giving feedback on a particular piece of work,
     it is best to wait as long as possible.   TRUE/FALSE

   d When giving feedback it is best to focus on specific
     situations rather than performance in general.   TRUE/FALSE

3 Which of the following are dangers involved in delegation, and why?

   a That jobs will be delegated for things which the team leader
      must retain personal responsibility for – such as safety.   ❐

   b That jobs will be delegated which everyone finds boring and
      unrewarding.   ❐

   c That team members will not carry out the jobs correctly.   ❐

   d That a team member will find the new job so rewarding that
      he or she will lose interest in other work.   ❐

4 List three ways in which a team member might be given more
   control over the work she or he does.   ❐

   _____

   _____

   _____

Answers to these questions can be found on pages 118–19.

7 Summary

- To know what motivates team members, you have to **get to know them.**

- **Organizations** can provide the means to help satisfy all levels of needs of employees.

- The team leader can implement the ideas of **motivation** and **job enrichment** by
  - helping to engender the right climate;
  - providing appropriate rewards;
  - enriching jobs.

- Using agreed **SMART objectives** can help your team's motivation.

- **Job enrichment** can entail
  - delegating tasks;
  - providing feedback;
  - giving team members more scope.

Performance checks

▪ 1 Quick quiz

Write down your answers in the space below to the following questions on *Managing Performance*.

Question 1   If a product has to be perfectly spherical, how might you measure the extent to which the required standard is met over a period of time?

_____

_____

Question 2   Give four examples of connected stakeholders.

_____

_____

Question 3   Who decides what is acceptable performance?

_____

_____

Question 4   Why should performance standards be quantified wherever possible?

_____

_____

Question 5   When might a standard be revised?

_____

_____

Question 6 What is meant by job enlargement? Give a brief description in your own words.

_____

_____

Question 7 Now define job rotation, briefly.

_____

_____

Question 8 What is a SMART objective?

_____

_____

Question 9 Which kind of jobs lend themselves most readily to job enrichment?

_____

_____

Question 10 Name three ways in which you can have ongoing communication with staff regarding their performance.

_____

_____

Question 11 What is the most basic principle about giving negative feedback?

_____

_____

Question 12 We have used the term 'autonomy', without defining it. How would you explain what it means?

_____

_____

Question 13 Make three suggestions to someone who asks: 'How can I motivate my staff?'

_____

_____

Answers to these questions can be found on pages 120–1.

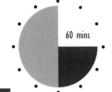

2 Workbook assessment

Read the following case incident and then deal with the questions that follow. Write your answers on a separate sheet of paper.

Nicole Petty worked at the head office of a travel company for ten years. Initially she found the work exciting and demanding but the pressures of work were very high. She was earning a good salary by the travel industry standards, but was becoming increasingly frustrated with the heavy work load.

When asked to manage a new travel agency office in Torquay, Nicole jumped at the chance, seeing this as an opportunity to spend less time on administration and more on 'being a travel agent'.

Nicole engaged three members of staff – two counter clerks, Jenny Downs and Darryl Proven, and an administrative assistant, Shanin Ahmed.

Nicole decided that she would organize the agency on a specialist basis as far as possible. All clients requiring an individual holiday would be referred to her and Nicole would design a package especially for them. This was the most difficult and interesting part of the work. However, she decided to let Jenny take care of the administrative side of these holidays. Nicole also decided to handle all business travel enquiries personally.

Darryl was to specialize in package holidays, while Jenny was to look after air, rail, coach and ferry reservations and ticketing, together with car hire and independent hotel bookings. Issues related to passports, visas, foreign currency, traveller's cheques and travel insurance were dealt with by both counter clerks.

The counter staff were obliged to enter all transactions in a central filing system for easy reference. Shanin was responsible for ensuring that information was correctly filed, although she spent most of her time on other clerical duties and word processing correspondence dictated by Nicole and the two counter clerks. All letters were checked and signed by Nicole.

Prizes and incentives earned by the counter clerks for the sale of special offer package tours were pooled and redistributed equally between Jenny, Darryl and Shanin at the end of each month.

After three months of operation, Nicole reviewed the performance of the agency and was not pleased with what she found. Absenteeism was increasing and the timekeeping of the staff had deteriorated. A number of customers had complained about the 'off-hand manner' of the counter staff and about the quality of service in general. Some customers had even complained about the quality of the typed correspondence. Nicole approached her employees and expressed her concern. She was surprised to learn that all three were not happy with their wages and Darryl also added that he was bored with the job.

Nicole promised to review their wages and hinted that they would all receive a reasonable pay rise.

You only need to write **two** or **three** sentences in response to each question.

1 How could Nicole go about introducing job enrichment in the travel agency?

2 What would be the likely effects of introducing job enrichment?

3 Describe the job changes Nicole might make to enrich the jobs of the two counter clerks.

4 Advise Nicole as to any other changes she could make that might improve motivation.

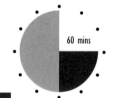

3 Work-based assignment

The time guide for this assignment gives you an approximate idea of how long it is likely to take you to write up your findings. You will find you need to spend some additional time gathering information, talking to colleagues, and thinking about the assignment.

In this workbook we have discussed some ideas for enriching jobs. For this assignment, you should consider how job enrichment might be applied to the work of one member of your team.

This Assignment may provide the basis of appropriate evidence for your S/NVQ portfolio. It is designed to help you to demonstrate your ability to motivate your team to improve their performance.

What you have to do

1 Select a job you feel would benefit from job enrichment.

2 Provide a brief description of the job as it now exists.

3 Describe, briefly, the changes you would like to see made to enrich the job. Explain how each change you've recommended would contribute to the process.

4 Then consider the expected effects of carrying out this plan – on the job, on the person concerned, on you and on the rest of the team.

Reflect and review

1 Reflect and review

Now that you have completed your work on *Managing Performance*, let us review our workbook objectives.

The first objectives were:

- that you should be better able to identify ways of measuring performance levels; and
- that you should be better able to describe a range of methods for measuring performance.

Performance measures should always be considered in relation to something: usually past performance, desired or expected future performance or the performance of something or somebody else.

You can judge the quality of performance using terms like 'delicious', but this may mean different things to different people. It is far better to use quantitative measures, because these give you a clear target to aim for and hopefully beat. Quantitative measures can be subdivided into financial measures (budgets and variances) and non-financial measures (times, weights, units of product or service, and so on).

Performance might also be measured against the economy in general or against the performance of competitors. Benchmarking is a useful technique: this compares performance with 'best in class' competitors or other departments.

- By what means is the performance of your work team measured at present? Do you have budgetary targets, or time deadlines to meet, or a target number of things to process per day/week/month? If you just cope as best you can with unpredictable daily demand, suggest some ways in which you could take control by making more effort to measure various aspects of performance.

_____

_____

_____

_____

_____

_____

■ Do you know who is regarded as 'best in class' at what they do? If not, find out, and make a note of ways you could discover more about how they operate (e.g. buy their products and experience their performance levels for yourself).

_____

_____

_____

_____

_____

_____

The next workbook objective was:

■ that you should be better able to identify the differing objectives of stakeholders in the organization

Stakeholders can be divided into three types: internal stakeholders (employees), connected stakeholders (customers, suppliers, financiers), and external stakeholders (the government, the community). Each of these has their own objectives and they will judge the performance of you and your work team accordingly.

■ Describe your own stake in your organization.

_____

_____

_____

_____

_____

_____

- Who are your internal customers and suppliers, and what are their objectives?

  _____

  _____

  _____

  _____

  _____

  _____

The next objective was

- You should be better able to identify and agree performance objectives with the members of your work team.

  One way of motivating both the team and its individual members is to establish clear objectives for them. To ensure objectives are clear, make them SMART – that is, specific, measurable, achievable, relevant and timebound. Don't try to draw up objectives without the involvement of the person or people they are intended for – if the objectives are to act as motivators, they must arise out of a process of discussion. They must also relate to organizational goals and objectives.

  - What are the organizational goals that I must take into account when drawing up team and individual objectives?

    _____

    _____

    _____

  Finally, from your reading and understanding of the workbook, you are (we hope) better informed than you were. Your head is no doubt brimming with ideas about motivating the people who report to you. You may be sceptical of some of the theory and the ideas we've discussed, but you could do worse than try to apply them.

  - The following are the ideas which I intend to try out, in an effort to improve the motivation of my team members.

    _____

    _____

    _____

The next workbook objective was:

■ that you should be better able to select the ideal performance measure.

There is no single performance measure that suits everybody: it depends on who you are describing performance to and what their stake in the organization is. So the ideal way of measuring performance is the balanced scorecard approach, which considers performance from a variety of perspectives and tries to satisfy everyone.

■ Note down conflicts in the objectives of the different stakeholders in your part of the organization.

_____

_____

_____

_____

_____

_____

■ Now look at the list you have made above and decide who should win, from the point of view of your organization as a whole. (For instance, if your team wants less work and more pay, will that help your organization complete a job on time and within cost, and get more work in the future?) When you've done this, you should be able to prioritize the various performance measures that are applied to your department. Write a list, in order of importance, below.

_____

_____

_____

_____

_____

_____

The next workbook objective was:

■ that you should be better able to monitor performance against agreed targets.

To monitor performance you first need to decide what 'performance' actually means (by asking your stakeholders) and then quantify the key measures that demonstrate whether you are performing well or badly. An initial performance 'standard' can be set by finding out what is the average current performance. You will then aim to achieve or beat that standard all the time, not just some of the time. Monitoring will identify 'exceptions' – occasions when you failed to meet the standard – and you should investigate the reasons why this happened.

■ Non-financial information is very useful for investigating failures, but you have to have the information in the first place. What records do you and your work team currently keep that could be used in performance measurement? Don't forget to include things that are recorded automatically, like the dates of computer files.

_____

_____

_____

_____

_____

_____

■ Make a list of items of additional information about the activities of your work team that you *could* record, and then go through the list deciding whether it is actually worth recording that information. In other words, decide whether the benefits of having the information outweigh the cost (probably time) of recording it and analysing it.

_____

_____

_____

_____

_____

_____

The final workbook objective was:

■ that you should be better able to make recommendations for improvement in performance, or adjustments to more realistic targets.

Targets can't always be met, often because of circumstances beyond your control. If this is the case, the most important thing is to tell the people you are going to let down as early as possible, and agree a new target that you will be able to meet.

As a general rule, however, businesses should aim to improve continuously, and many adopt organization-wide initiatives such as Total Quality Management or ISO 9000 certification to achieve this.

When looking for areas of improvement, it is helpful to think in terms of inputs, processes and outputs. Think especially about whether things you currently do need to be done at all, whether you can integrate processes (combine them into one) or automate them somehow, and whether you can address people issues such as training and relationships with other departments.

■ What improvements have you made since you took charge of your work team? Make a note below, and concentrate on things that are quantified.

_____

_____

_____

_____

_____

_____

■ What improvements do the stakeholders in your part of the organization want to see in the future – over the next six months say? If you don't know, ask them (your staff, your own manager, your colleagues in other departments) and make a note of their responses below.

_____

_____

_____

_____

_____

_____

▪ 2 Action plan

Use this plan to further develop for yourself a course of action you want to take. Make a note in the left-hand column of the issues or problems you want to tackle, and then decide what you intend to do, and make a note in column 2.

The resources you need might include time, materials, information or money. You may need to negotiate for some of them, but they could be something easily acquired, like half an hour of somebody's time, or a chapter of a book. Put whatever you need in column 3. No plan means anything without a timescale, so put a realistic target completion date in column 4.

Finally, describe the outcome you want to achieve as a result of this plan, whether it is for your own benefit or advancement, or a more efficient way of doing things.

Desired outcomes				
1 Issues	2 Action	3 Resources	4 Target completion
Actual outcomes				

3 Extensions

Extension 1

Book	*Balanced Scorecard Step-by-Step: Maximizing Performance and Maintaining Results*
Authors	Paul R Niven and Robert S Kaplan
Edition	2002
Publisher	John Wiley & Sons

This book explains how an organization can measure and manage performance with the balanced scorecard methodology. It provides extensive background on performance management and the balanced scorecard, and focuses on guiding a team through the step-by-step development and ongoing implementation of a balanced scorecard system. It's also available as an e-book.

Extension 2

Book	*101 Ways to Improve Business Performance*
Author	Donald Waters
Edition	1999
Publisher	Kogan Page

This book describes ideas for improving business performance, taking the view that the purpose of every organization is to make a product that satisfies customer needs. The text examines management support, product design, quality management, planning, equipment and logistics.

Extension 3

Book	*Understanding Organizations*
Author	Charles B. Handy
Edition	4th edition, 1999
Publisher	Penguin Books

A general book on organizations, written by the famous Professor Handy, who has vast experience in the management field. The chapter called 'On the motivation to work' is the most relevant to our subject.

These Extensions can be taken up via your ILM Centre. They will either have them or will arrange that you have access to them. However, it may be more convenient to check out the materials with your personnel or training people at work – they may well give you access. There are other good reasons for approaching your own people; for example, they will become aware of your interest and you can involve them in your development.

4 Answers to self-assessment questions

Self-assessment 1 on pages 32–3

1 Here is an analysis that shows the total production and how much each factory contributes to the total, as a percentage.

	Quarter 1	Quarter 2	Quarter 3	Quarter 4
Factory A	31,200 63%	31,000 62%	34,300 68%	29,800 48%
Factory B	18,500 37%	19,300 38%	16,200 32%	31,700 52%
	49,700	50,300	50,500	61,500

From this you can see that the overall production is reasonably consistent for the first three quarters (about 50,000 units), with Factory A doing most of the work.

In the fourth quarter, production shoots up by about 10,000 units and the two factories do an almost equal amount of work, although in fact it is only Factory B which increases production by a significant amount.

The most likely reason for this is that we are not comparing like with like for the first three quarters. Factory B was probably smaller or less well-equipped, or had some other problems that affected its ability to produce more than 20,000 units. By the time we get to the fourth quarter, Factory B seems to have been brought up to the standard of Factory A.

2 If people keep leaving your organization to go to another job that may be an indication that morale is not very good.

Staff turnover is calculated by dividing the number of leavers by the total number of staff. For instance, if you have a team of 12 people and three leave during the year and are replaced, you have a staff turnover of $3/12 \times 100\% = 25\%$.

If people don't like coming to work that may be because of low morale. Absenteeism is measured by comparing the number of days or hours lost in the year compared with the total number of hours that people should have worked.

Your own management activity can also be used as a measure. You could keep a record of the number of times you have to step in to resolve conflicts between members of your team.

Your team members will have their own views and you could ask them to rate morale on a scale of I to I0, say.

You may have had other valid ideas.

3 Benchmarking is a good way of avoiding COMPLACENCY and it may give rise to NEW IDEAS.

The main interest of shareholders is to get a RETURN on their INVEST-MENT, so PROFITABILITY is usually thought of as a commercial organization's prime objective.

The balanced scorecard looks at an organization from four different points of view.

a CUSTOMER
b INTERNAL
c INNOVATION AND LEARNING
d FINANCIAL

Self-assessment 2 on page 58

1 Your internal customers are the people, or groups of people, in your organization who need the work that you do to enable them to do their job.

2 An ideal standard is based on perfect operating conditions: no inefficiencies, no lost or wasted time, no machine breakdowns or computer crashes, no wasted or spoiled materials.

The disadvantage of an ideal standard is that it's almost impossible to achieve because not everything can be controlled. Staff will not be motivated to perform well if they can never reach the standard required.

3 a Monitoring performance is a way of keeping CONTROL over the activities you are responsible for.
b When there is a variance from expected performance you should use measures to see where ERRORS, FAILURES AND DEFECTS occurred.

4 The most important thing is to be totally open about it. You should tell everyone who relies on your department's performance at the earliest opportunity that you won't meet your targets. This gives them the opportunity to make alternative arrangements.

5 Improvement should be continuous because:

■ if you just stand still your competitors will come out with a better product and take your share of the market;
■ technology is changing and advancing faster than ever before, creating new opportunities and making old ways of doing things obsolete;
■ customers have come to expect higher and higher quality.

6 Here are three possible ways to improve processes (other answers may be equally valid).

■ Integrate with other processes.
■ Automate routine tasks.
■ Consider whether they can be eliminated completely.

Self-assessment 3 on page 71

1 The principle behind the MICRO-DIVISION OF LABOUR is that jobs are broken down into the SMALLEST possible elements.

2 Job enrichment means designing jobs so that people have more SKILL VARIETY, TASK IDENTITY, AUTONOMY, TASK SIGNIFICANCE, and FEEDBACK FROM THE JOB. (In no particular order.)

3 JOB ROTATION involves switching people between a number of different jobs of relatively similar COMPLEXITY.

4 JOB ENLARGEMENT involves adding more TASKS of similar complexity to the job.

5 When jobs are broken down into very simple tasks that anyone can learn, the problem of staff turnover becomes unimportant: you 'just recruit more people off the street'. This is TRUE – if the organization is prepared to live with high levels of staff turnover.

6 Job enrichment is very hard to implement, because it entails lots of training to do more complex tasks. This is SOMETIMES TRUE: the amount of training required depends on the people doing the job. Often, job enrichment involves no training.

7 Job enrichment programmes should be presented as opportunities, not demands. This is TRUE.

8 Small organizations can't implement job enrichment programmes, as they do not have the resources of large companies. This is FALSE.

9 The following ideas support the concept of job enrichment:

a Herzberg's theory that job interest is a motivator.

d McGregor's Theory Y: that people prefer to control themselves than be controlled from above.

e Hackman and Oldham's theories about the prerequisites for internal motivation.

Self-assessment 4 on pages 98–9

1 a 'Get to know your team members well.' is GOOD advice, because no two people are the same – we all have our little quirks.

b 'Try to improve their working conditions.' is GOOD advice **only** if working conditions are so bad that morale has deteriorated.

c 'Give them more scope and more involvement.' is GOOD advice because the opportunity to develop is often one of the major attractions of the job.

d 'Watch them more closely, so they know you care about them.' is generally bad advice; this is the opposite of increasing autonomy.

2 a This statement is FALSE. A SMART objective is specific rather than short.

   b This statement is TRUE. One-to-one meetings are by far the best way of maintaining ongoing communication.

   c This statement is FALSE. It is in fact best to give feedback immediately after a particular piece of work has been completed rather than wait for any length of time.

   d This statement is TRUE. Feedback is more useful and better received if it focuses on specific situations rather than being general and vague.

3 ALL these can be said to be dangers involved in delegation, to some extent:

   a That jobs will be delegated for things which the team leader must retain personal responsibility for – such as safety. This **is** a danger, because there are some jobs which the team leader can't afford to delegate.

   b That jobs will be delegated which everyone finds boring and unrewarding. This **is** a danger, because it won't enrich anyone's work.

   c That team members will not carry out the jobs correctly. This **is** a danger, if the leader doesn't give proper instruction, or doesn't monitor performance.

   d That a team member will find the new job so rewarding that he or she will lose interest in other work. – This **is** a danger, and one which, in a sense is a danger of all job enrichment. Obviously, if people are to develop, they will want to progress to more interesting work.

4 You may have included:

- controlling the pace of the work;
- determining the order or sequence in which the work is done;
- deciding how the work is done;
- deciding when the work is done;
- choosing the tools, equipment or materials used for the job;
- influencing the quality of work produced;
- deciding where the work is done.

 # 5 Answers to activities

Activity 41 on pages 74–5

A possible set of answers is given in the following table. You may have included some that are more relevant to your own organization.

Physiological

- Canteen facilities
- Sleeping bags and tents
- Survival packs
- Drinking fountains
- Rest rooms
- Coffee breaks

Safety

- Safe working conditions
- Protective clothing
- First aid kits
- Pension and sick pay schemes
- Agreements on work procedures

Love

- The chance to work in a group
- Social clubs, etc.
- The opportunity to help others
- Rest rooms and canteen facilities where people can meet

Esteem

- Praise for work done
- Status symbols
- Recognition as a valued employee
- Job title and its associated authority
- Self-respect from achieving success at work

Self-actualization

- Interesting work
- The chance to be creative
- Challenging work
- The chance to develop skills and talents

6 Answers to the quick quiz

Answer 1   Measure the number of defective products: for instance three out of every 100 produced are not of the required quality.

Answer 2   Shareholders, suppliers, customers, financiers.

Answer 3   Stakeholders decide, especially customers.

Answer 4   If you have a numerical measure you have a very clear target to aim for and, if possible, beat.

Answer 5   When changes of a permanent nature occur, but not in response to temporary 'blips'. For example, the standard time for doing a task using a certain piece of equipment might change when a new version of the equipment is acquired.

Answer 6   Job enlargement means giving more tasks of similar complexity.

Answer 7   Job rotation is giving people a variety of jobs of the same complexity.

Answer 8   A SMART objective is one that is specific, measurable, achievable, and time bound.

Answer 9   Jobs where job satisfaction is low; maintenance factors are costly; changes would not be expensive; lack of motivation is affecting performance.

Answer 10   Ways of having ongoing communication with staff include regular written reports, team meetings, one-to-one meetings, and informal conversations with staff as part of 'management by walking around'.

Answer 11   The most basic principle about giving negative feedback is to balance it with some positive feedback.

Answer 12   Autonomy is 'self-government': the authority to do your job as you see fit.

Answer 13   You could have mentioned quite a number of things, including: following the principles of job enrichment; aiming to get the right kind of atmosphere; valuing effort and personal contribution; promoting the intrinsic worth of the job; making work fun.

7 Certificate

Completion of this certificate by an authorized person shows that you have worked through all the parts of this workbook and satisfactorily completed the assessments. The certificate provides a record of what you have done that may be used for exemptions or as evidence of prior learning against other nationally certificated qualifications.